HOW TO READ AND WRITE ABOUT DRAMA

GARY VENA, Ph.D.

Associate Professor at Manhattan College

ARCO
New York

Second Edition

Copyright © 1988 by Gary Vena

First Edition copyright © 1966 by Simon & Schuster

 ARCO

Simon & Schuster, Inc.
Gulf + Western Building
One Gulf + Western Plaza
New York, NY 10023

DISTRIBUTED BY PRENTICE HALL TRADE

Manufactured in the United States of America

1 2 3 4 5 6 7 8 9 10

Library of Congress Cataloging-in-Publication Data

Vena, Gary, 1942–
   How to read and write about drama / by Gary Vena. —2nd ed.
     p. cm.
   Bibliography: p.
   ISBN 0-
   1. Dra
PN1707.V46 1988
808.2—dc19   88-14158
                          CIP

TABLE OF CONTENTS

Perspectives of the Drama 5; Spectator Sportsmanship and the Classical Drama 6; Aristotle and the Tragedians 8; Classicism and the Unities 8; Greek Tragedy versus Comedy 9; Roman Drama 9; Medieval Drama 10; Drama and Contemporary Ritual 11; Elizabethan Drama 12; Restoration Drama 14; Eighteenth- and Nineteenth-Century Drama 15; Romanticism 15; Melodrama and the Well-Made Play 16; Stepping into the Twentieth Century 17; Origins of African Drama 19; Popular and Literary versus Folk and Primitive 20; Influences of Music and Dance 20; Contemporary Black American Drama 21; Asian Drama 23; Japanese Performance Styles 24; Themes for Analysis: Theatre History 25.

Classical Greek Drama 31; Classical Roman Comedy 33; Roman Comedy and the *Commedia Dell'arte* 33; Medieval Drama 36; Elizabethan Drama 37; Restoration and Eighteenth-Century Drama 40; Realistic Drama of the Late Nineteenth and Early Twentieth Centuries 41; Theatre Companies versus Stage Characters 43; Realistic Drama of the Mid-Twentieth Century 44; Themes for Analysis: Characters 45.

What to Listen For 49; Themes for Analysis: Hearing Stage Characters 59.

CHAPTER FOUR
SETTING THE STAGE FOR ACTION   61

The Dramatis Personae 61; Symbolic Nomenclature 62; Character and Stage Descriptions 63; The Simple Setting 64; Altering Stage Realism 65; Expressionism 66; Realism, Symbolism, and Dramatic Foreshadowing 67; Character as Key to Setting 68; Musical Sound Effects 70; Noisy Sound Effects 71; Costume Effects 72; Dressing for Status 73; Dressing for Mood 73; Dressing for Theatrical Effects 74; Themes for Analysis: Setting the Stage 75.

CHAPTER FIVE
DRAMATIC STRUCTURES   79

What Is Plot? 79; The Aristotelian (Dramatic) Model 80; What Is the Deus ex Machina? 81; Discovering the Theme 82; Aristotle and the Elizabethans 82; Plot versus Dramatic Irony 83; Analogous Actions 83; Plot versus Subplot 84; Plotting the Well-Made Play 85; Comedy versus Farce versus Black Comedy 86; The Brechtian (Epic) Model 86; Brecht's Model in Action 87; Approaching the Brechtian Model 88; Discovering Brecht's Influence 89; The Brechtian Model versus the Non-Brecht Play 90; Mainstream versus Alternative: The *Eclectic* Model 91; Artaud and the Theatre of Cruelty 92; Experiencing the Eclectic Model 92; Responding to the "Environmental" Process 94; Background to a Feminist Aesthetic 95; Art versus Gender 95; Aristotle's Antifeminist Aesthetic 96; Hellman and the Prefeminist Drama 97; What Is Feminist Theatre? 97; Churchill's Radical Model 99; Drawing Some Possible Conclusions 101; Themes for Analysis: Dramatic Structures 102.

CHAPTER SIX
LANGUAGE: THE KEY TO CHARACTER AND ACTION   105

Language as Subtext 106; Achieving a Poetry *of* the Theatre 108; The Uses of Dramatic Irony 110; Wordplay, Double-Entendre, and the Language of Comedy 112; The Art of Rhyming Couplets 113; Elitist

CHAPTER SEVEN
APPROACHING THE *MISE-EN-SCÈNE*   139

GLOSSARY   *167*

SUGGESTED READING   *177*

ACKNOWLEDGMENTS

For J. R. S.

INTRODUCTION
IN DEFENSE OF PLAYREADING

The play's the thing,
Wherein I'll catch the conscience of the king!
—*Hamlet*, II, ii

One of the great stage designers of our century, Robert Edmond Jones, insists that "the loveliest and most poignant of all stage pictures are those that are seen in the mind's eye." His words have much in common with Hamlet's advice to the players, as they describe the playreader's task precisely, especially today when we seem less called upon to exercise the powers of theatrical imagination. The universal popularity of spectator sports, pop music videos, televised courtroom hearings, flashy computer games, larger-than-life evangelists, and the countless other events and rituals of everyday life frequently determines the repertory of images we are capable of integrating. In an age of ever higher technology, state-of-the-art merchandising, and computer literacy, it becomes increasingly difficult to reserve those quieter corners of our imagination, as society seduces its members to "plug into" the media events that surround them. We are assaulted from all sides.

In such a time and place, the lively arts of music, film, dance, and drama have needed to redefine themselves for survival. Of course, this process is not peculiar to the twentieth century. History has repeatedly witnessed artistic upheavals through which newer energies and styles have emerged. In the world of drama, for example, such conflicts have produced many enduring theatre pieces, or "classics." The drama of ancient Greece was generated through fierce playwriting competitions, from which precious few samples have survived. The early Christian church terminated the act of drama, which it deemed immoral, only to revive it centuries later upon its sacred medieval altars. In modern times, the rigid and stylized Kabuki struggles to retain meaning in a newly industrialized Japan, four centuries after its inception. A new

1

worldwide technology has inspired a bolder "alternative theatre" movement to topple the traditional approaches to drama. Our study will focus on many of these examples in our effort to understand and appreciate their literary and performance values. We recognize drama as a genre that not only flourishes on conflict and survives in spite of it but also produces a body of work that consistently challenges "the mind's eye."

Living in a technological society can be an advantage for an informed playreader who chooses to analyze and write about drama. Performances are available at all times, in many places. A pedestrian can adjust his earphones and plug into a Beethoven sonata or rock concert as he marches along. Through the magic of instant replay, a sports fan can analyze the strategy of two opponents in the arena. A video rental will allow the viewer to experience a play by Tennessee Williams and an opera by Guiseppe Verdi, all in the same evening. Sophisticated computer programming effortlessly transforms the playreader into a stage director by enabling him to manipulate Shakespeare's characters displayed before him on the computer screen. Some cite disadvantages to this automatic accessibility, claiming that it diminishes intelligent internal responses, turning its users into passive recipients of indiscriminate sound and light waves. Others bemoan such mechanical overdependence as one cause of illiteracy.

Whatever the arguments, however, tradition demands a literary script, which it equates fairly or not with drama: the playwright creates his play; the playreader reads it. If the playwright is lucky, his or her play will be "staged"—that is, brought to life by actors. Just as the play is defined through its characters and actions, playreading—rather than playgoing—emerges as the more available medium through which we discover the play. Thus, the skillful art of playreading always needs nurturing, prompting our adherence to a special set of criteria to determine what constitutes "good theatre." For it is the play that ultimately inspires our imagination by holding "the mirror up to nature," as Hamlet exclaims.

"How to read and write about drama." Is this lively art and literary genre so unique as to require its own methods of analysis? The answer is yes. The dramatic event first takes shape in the mind of the playwright who uses language—an assortment of verbal and nonverbal clues—to structure the story and to enhance our understanding of the characters and situations set before us. Behind this theatrical illusion is a tangible reality rooted in the language of the play. So we had best ignore the tired notion that the drama can find life *only* on the stage, and recognize instead that palpable theatrical life exists on the printed page if we are prepared to discover it. A short historical view of Western drama serves as a reliable starting point.

CHAPTER ONE
WHAT STAGE HISTORY TELLS US

All the world's a stage,
And all the men and women merely players.
—*As You Like It*, II, vii

Perspectives of the Drama

Shakespeare's metaphor, spoken by a melancholy Jaques, remains a timely one, especially in Western drama where a continuing tradition has connected the numerous stages of dramatic history. Let us think of it as a ladderlike vertical force that ties certain contemporary plays to their classical origins. In turn, the modern theatre has successfully revived the classical models, finding profound relevance in their form and content, and discovering that they still speak for themselves. The fascination for earlier traditions is not simply rooted in bookish curiosity or the need to introduce modern audiences to classical styles. Despite their religious origins in the worship of Dionysus, the exciting language, strong characters, and compelling plots of the ancient Greek drama have always been popular with contemporary Western audiences. These plays still challenge inventive theatre directors to discover innovative approaches to presenting them.

During a time of greater global awareness of cultural variety, this vertical perspective has been enhanced by a horizontal one, encouraging Western critics to view the theatrical performances of their neighbors from other continents. The incorporation of urgent anthropological issues, aided by an intense study of significant performance styles, has finally broadened the traditional Western view. Such cross-cultural exchanges have enriched the viewers. A Western audience can relish the traditional Kathakali dance theatre of India or the work of African playwrights and performers in much the same way that audiences in Shanghai and Beijing can attend performances of plays by such American stalwarts as Eugene O'Neill and Arthur Miller.

Spectator Sportsmanship and the Classical Drama

Assuming the contemporary playreader has vast theatrical resources to plug into, including a tradition of amply documented Western drama, the similarities to earlier traditions appear far greater than any contrasts. Take, for example, the modern sports event where fans participate in a variety of experiences that on close consideration parallel the drama festivals of ancient Greece, where the rules for Western drama were born.

Let us consider some of these parallels. Today's sports figures usually undergo an out-of-town season of heavy practice sessions, building energy and stamina, perfecting their movements and strategies, and striving to function as one harmonious team. *Classical actors also rehearsed vigorously, strengthening their vocal and physical powers as individual actors or members of the chorus but always working together to become a total acting ensemble.*

Today's spectator sits in the open air, often in the daylight, among thousands of fans. The setting is a vast stadium, circular in shape, with gradually elevated rows of seats surrounding the sports figures who present their strategies at center. *His classical counterpart viewed the drama, starting at dawn, with an audience of twenty thousand townspeople. The ancient theatre at Epidaurus, one of many built along the Grecian hillsides, was semicircular or horseshoelike in design, with similarly elevated rows of seats chiseled out of stone. These surrounded the actors who performed in a circular space, called the "orchestra," far below.*

Today the sports fan seeks out the one set of offensive or defensive "players" he personally values as worthy of attention, a favorite team he then cheers on to win. He applauds the dexterous maneuvers of the team's star players, as they overwhelm their villainous opposition and strive toward a victorious outcome. *His classical counterpart beheld the words and gestures of characters who, highlighted against a chorus, moved through a series of connected actions toward some unexpected fate. A leading actor played the protagonist, the hero who supported a universal good. He won the playgoer's sympathy as he overcame the villainy of his antagonist, whose maneuvers blocked his desired victory.*

The sports event provides its fans with action-packed moments and split-second countdowns in which the fate of one team is at the mercy of the other. The pace quickens, then drops, depending on the impulses of emotionally and physically charged players and the supportive cheers from the grandstand. *In the ancient drama festival, peaks of emotion frequently surfaced and subsided, sweeping over an awestruck audience, signaling the rising and falling actions of the drama. The actors, their faces hidden behind expressive masks, knew they had won the playgoers' sympathy.*

Fans at the stadium ventilate their stored emotions vicariously through the actions of the players on the field. The score is tied, and precious few seconds remain in the game. A favorite player scores the winning point as the final few seconds tick away. The fans go wild. *At the theatre of Epidaurus, the actors built toward one particular moment, the highest point of their respective actions, where the fate of the antagonist took a negative turn, assuring the protagonist's success: the inevitable climax followed by the final unraveling, or denouement, as Western audiences have called it.*

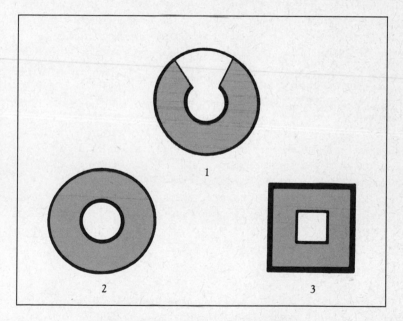

1

2 3

The circular design of the classical Greek theatre (Fig. 1) characterizes today's adaptable sports arena as well as the contemporary "theatre-in-the-round" and "arena-stage" designs (Figs. 2 and 3). (Shaded area indicates the audience.)

This sense of purge or renewal, known as *katharsis* in Greek drama, proves uplifting to both sports fans and playgoers alike and provides a needed emotional *completion* to the "high drama" experienced. Finally, both sets of spectators return to their homes and villages with a unified perspective that these events *occurred in a single block of real time, were contained in one setting, and were played out to their completion.*

Aristotle and the Tragedians

This brief overview reminds us how much modern spectators share with their classical counterparts and, more important, how they have learned to structure such impressions against those concepts first introduced by the Greek philosopher Aristotle (384–322 B.C.). In his famous *Theory of Poetry*, popularly called the *Poetics*, Aristotle devised a framework for viewing literature, notably the drama, which he documented through a careful analysis of certain performances he attended at the drama festivals in ancient Greece. The playwrights whose works he observed were all writers of tragedy: Aeschylus (525–456 B.C.), an original master of style and spectacle who wrote more than ninety plays and won the heralded playwriting prize on thirteen separate occasions; Sophocles (496–406 B.C.), the dramatic poet who uncovered universal truths in his exploration of mankind's myths; and Euripides (486–406 B.C.), renowned for his psychological insights and strong female characters. For better or worse, Aristotle's treatise, devised after the deaths of these writers, has had a profound effect on Western literary tradition, offering both the playwright and the critic a dynamic set of criteria against which to build, as well as criticize, a work of literary art.

Classicism and the Unities

There is one Aristotelian concept especially worth noting: the rule of the *Three Unities*. In his theory Aristotle recommended that every work of art should be unified by its subject or theme. Indeed, subsequent interpretations of his rule evolved into three separate unities of action, time, and place. A play should tell a single story; it should happen in a single day and be presented in a single scene. The rule has challenged playwrights and theatre practitioners through many centuries. It has, as the contemporary reader will observe, left its mark on the most elementary lesson in style: the need for a literary work to have a beginning, a middle, and an end. This formal design, which sought to produce balance, proportion, and restraint, evolved into an important literary style known as *classicism*.

Greek Tragedy versus Comedy

Rooted in religious ritual and the worship of the god Dionysus, the typical Greek tragedy adhered to Aristotle's classical design. The tragedy traced the protagonist's rise to some prominent height, the clashing of wills in his struggle against his antagonist, and his disastrous fall.

Conversely, the Greeks did not lack an appetite for humor, as the many extant comedies of Aristophanes (450–385 B.C.) prove. Aristophanes's skills as playwright and satirist incorporated a variety of political, literary, and sexual targets. He elevated the art of comedy to a level commensurate with tragedy. In his *Poetics*, Aristotle had very little to say about this important form of drama, which celebrated man's triumph over the calamities and downfalls of his life. Like tragedy, comic drama was rooted in ritual, except that renewal and rebirth defined a happy, as opposed to darker, purpose. More important, our historical perspective shows that the comedies of Aristophanes would always remain inseparable—in form and content—from the comic traditions they spawned.

Roman Drama

The classical Roman drama deserves our careful consideration for three reasons: (1) its alteration and more flexible usage of the physical stage; (2) its variety of popular stage characters; and (3) its form and content as impetus to the later medieval drama. Regarding the first of these, in the same way that the playing field of contemporary sports stadiums can accommodate varying audience arrangements, the Romans reduced the circular performance sphere of the Greek theatre to a semicircle, allowing select playgoers to be seated in the *orchestra*, a term still used by Western audiences. Eventually, Roman actors would perform in still smaller auditoriums and on raised stages carefully separated from the spectators. For the thrill-seekers, however, the existence of the famous Colosseum, built about 75 A.D., reflected the

Roman theatregoers' taste for large-scale extravaganzas, many of which have been exaggerated, if not exactly recreated, in countless Hollywood films. Whereas Greek audiences thrived on tragedy, the Romans craved comedy. Two Roman playwrights named Plautus (254–184 B.C.) and Terence (190–159 B.C.) not only embellished the earlier Aristophanic tradition but also established newer ones. Their sharp crackling dialogue, rich caricatures, and comical plots spiced with musical interludes transformed the Western tradition of comedy forever.

The classical playwright who closes our view of the Roman drama is Seneca (3 B.C.–65 A.D.). Unlike his colleagues, Plautus and Terence, Seneca wrote tragedies characterized by a rigid, artificial literary style and a blood-and-gore content that appealed to the jaded tastes of the declining Roman empire. After Seneca the tradition of literary drama quietly disappeared. Gladiatorial and nautical spectacles continued to fascinate Roman spectators until the fifth century A.D., when the hostility of the Christian church terminated all forms of theatre.

Medieval Drama

The death of the classical era put an end to these larger-than-life physical stagings. Open-air performances with massive audiences, requiring stylized gestures and artificially projected voices, were suddenly part of the historical past. In the interim, clowns, mimes, and acrobats carried their talents through the Dark Ages of medieval Europe, from the fifth to the tenth centuries. At the dawn of the tenth century, however, the Christian church displaced the temple of Dionysus. The church, the institution that had halted all forms of theatre, was about to see drama reborn on its own sacred altars.

There is no little irony that the rebirth of drama was harmoniously in keeping with the Church's daily ritual of the Holy Mass. The occasion was simple enough: a small segment of chanted dialogue, called a *trope*, was incorporated into the ritual of the Mass, requiring the additional participation of two separate choruses. The script, retelling the story of several holy women and a group of angels whom they encounter at the tomb of the recently crucified Christ, contained enormous theatrical potential. Furthermore, the ornamental liturgical vestments worn by the priest and his celebrants theatrically embellished the chanted choral exchanges until in time the trope was extended into a full "liturgical" play.

From simple trope to full liturgical play, the plots were always based on the stories of the Old and New Testaments. The individual names of playwrights were never recorded. The scripts appeared to be collaborative efforts, that is, the contributions of many anonymous participants. Soon, medieval guilds were established, where members convened to sponsor, organize, and rehearse their plays. Chester, York, and Wakefield were just a few of the English towns that gave their names to the multiple episodes or mysteries (collectively called cycles) that emerged. The countless parishioners who assembled to view them could no longer be accommodated within the walls of these churches. So the medieval drama, which had originated upon sacred altars, was left with no other choice but to go public.

By the eleventh and twelfth centuries, the cycles developed through-out central Europe. Their appeal became twofold: not only did the plays entertain their audiences, but they also communicated solid lessons from the Bible to young and old alike, asserting that the purpose of drama could also be *didactic*, or instructive. Most of all, the medieval drama quickly established itself as a cooperative enterprise, incorporat-ing the energies and talents of many innovative theatre practitioners. In going public, the drama went out-of-doors. Primitive stage ma-chinery was spread across wide open fields, and earthen dugouts were employed for special effects. *Pageant wagons* were devised to transport the players and stage sets, also known as *mansions*, from one town to the next. The guilds conveniently unfolded their biblical stories, then packed up their stage properties to travel on. Often the wagons were positioned in a circle, allowing members of the audience to circulate from one play to another, to follow their connected but episodic reenactments. The desire to create drama became acceptable once more, and a fairly modern theatrical style developed.

Drama and Contemporary Ritual

As contemporary viewers, our imagination and experience can help us understand the development of medieval drama in Western Europe, which continued through the fifteenth century. Many of us have had the occasion to be present at some religious ceremony, whether in a church, synagogue, or mosque. The experience produces a strong sense of intimacy as the elected performers—priests, rabbis, or ministers— engage us in their stylized actions, appropriately known as *rituals*.

Depending on the occasion, of course, the nature of the religious service is changeable in its complexity and length. In many services, our participation is *vicarious*, that is, experienced through previously elected participants who represent the general congregation. However, with the lowering of lights, the addition of candles and incense, and musical accompaniment of any form, the religious ritual dramatically evolves into a theatrical experience, offering the congregation a sense of renewal not unlike the *katharsis* of the classical Greek drama. So an increased sense of ritual and community facilitates our appreciation and understanding of the earlier "stages" of the drama's development.

Elizabethan Drama

By the sixteenth century, the need to dramatize—or better yet, to *commercialize* drama—had become a conditioned reality, allowing both playwright and performer to recognize the professional possibilities of their crafts. Elizabethan drama, named after the ruling monarch, Elizabeth I, was unique in its contribution to the literature of the theatre. Noted primarily for the prolific contributions of its most popular playwright, William Shakespeare (1564–1616), the Elizabethan Age produced Christopher Marlowe, Thomas Kyd, and John Webster, as well as such later Stuart playwrights as Ben Jonson, Thomas Middleton, and John Ford. Among other innovations, these skilled craftsmen significantly modified the Aristotelian unities of time, place, and action, to suit their own needs and to accommodate more than one plot and multiple stage actions.

Compared with the classical and medieval stages, there are vast differences in the structure of the Globe Theatre, where Shakespeare's plays were performed. The theatre was octagonal in shape, and the actors performed on a large elevated rectangular platform that extended from one side of the octagon and was covered by an extended roof. Behind the platform stage there was a permanent wall that provided a natural backdrop or setting to the action. On this back wall there were two or three balcony-like levels that served as additional acting areas. More than fifteen hundred spectators sat on wooden benches that lined three roofed galleries surrounding the three sides of the platform. These *sightlines* provided the playgoer with an optimum view of the stage and established an *aesthetic distance*—a comfortable physical and emotional space between actor and spectator—which would leave its mark on the

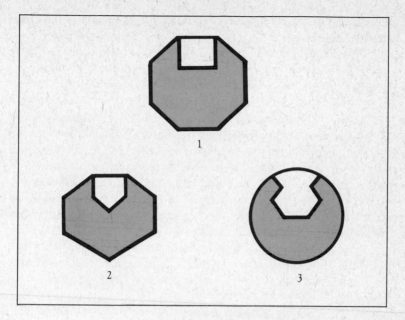

The octagonal Globe Theatre, with its stage prominently projected from one side (fig. 1), foreshadows modern theatre variations of the "thrust stage," which brought the actors closer to the audience (figs. 2 and 3). (Shaded area indicates the audience.)

modern theatre. For a few shillings, additional spectators (the "groundlings") could stand in an open yard or pit between the stage and the galleries.

Because the use of stage sets and props was minimal in the Elizabethan theatre, compared to its medieval counterpart, a greater responsibility was placed on the intelligence and imagination of the Elizabethan playgoer. In viewing the tragedies, comedies, and historical dramas of Shakespeare, for example, a typical playgoer was required to integrate certain physical and psychological aspects of the performance. The plays were performed by unmasked men, so there was greater emphasis on individual character development. Multiple scene shifts, reflecting the different physical settings within the play, were handled without the benefit of a stage curtain; and the blazing light of day could offer no *illusion* to scenes set at night. Above all, Shakespeare and his contemporaries relied on the spectator's imagination, with results that satisfied all expectations.

Restoration Drama

In contrast with Elizabethan theatre, which had served all classes of society, the newly emerged theatre of Restoration England became an exclusive entertainment, catering solely to court society and mirroring the intrigues and frivolities of its modish participants. Nevertheless, the Restoration period (1660–1688) remains a vital link in the vertical perspective of theatre history because of the modern conventions it demonstrated. Restoration drama revived the classical unities, which the Elizabethan playwrights largely ignored, thus establishing the beginnings of *neoclassicism*. In fact, many Restoration playwrights had little regard for the plays of the Elizabethans and established the unfortunate tradition of altering them, if not rewriting them completely.

Inspired, no doubt, by Shakespeare's rich comic canon, playwrights such as William Wycherley, William Congreve, and George Farquhar encountered great success with comedy. Their sharply etched characters, who bore such names as Lady Fidget, Quack, Mrs. Pinchwife, and Charles Surface, often found themselves in sexually compromising positions and could depend only on their acid-tongued wit for rescue. Their popularity left little room for writers of tragedy who found no lasting popularity with Restoration playgoers.

The Restoration playhouse evolved into a considerably more modern structure, much like the Broadway and London theatres operating today. It was a totally enclosed structure, employing candles and oil lamps to control house lighting and create stage illusion. But more important, the Restoration playhouse developed a total stage set, an elevated boxlike interior framed like a picture. The audience sat facing the stage, in a location comparable to the Elizabethan pit, but more stylishly furnished. Backless benches symmetrically lined the seating area, while boxes and *galleries*, also known as balconies, provided additional seating in later, more sophisticated structures.

In addition to these changes, women were for the first time prominently featured as legitimate, professional stage actresses, part of a flourishing star system that attracted enthusiastic fans. The theatrical environments of London and European cities saw the emergence of acting companies, theatre managers, and other professionals who cared about the production of plays, as well as the financial possibilities of the theatre. So supportive was the system, as a matter of fact, that London witnessed the appearance of its first successful female playwright, Aphra Behn.

Eighteenth- and Nineteenth-Century Drama

By the beginning of the eighteenth century, however, the prominence of theatrical activity once again dwindled, not so much in the quantity of production but in its quality. While the writing of great plays degenerated into sentimental comedies, domestic tragedies, bourgeois drama that focused on lower-class characters, and other forms of popular entertainment, the century became renowned for its great actors, such as David Garrick and Sarah Kemble Siddons, whose talents were carefully showcased. Theatres grew larger, box seats remained popular, and innovative and spectacular stage effects continued to hold the spectator's attention. English acting companies toured the American colonies in performances of their classics and before long inspired the beginnings of theatre in America.

Romanticism

By the nineteenth century, fantasy, romance, comedy, and melodrama were familiar words to the playgoer. A breakdown in the divisions of tragedy and comedy, as well as a staunch disregard for the classical unities, had surfaced during the last quarter of the eighteenth century. The new playwrights from France, Germany, and Italy were called *Romantics*, and their plays often depicted extravagant situations that would have been more comfortably suited to the format of a novel. *Romanticism* as a major literary style emphasized character and emotion above everything else, as demonstrated in the dramas of Schiller, Hugo, and Dumas *fils*. Seeking to create a drama that was individual, spontaneous, and even fantastic, these playwrights refused to conform with reality. The style lasted through a good part of the nineteenth century, during which time some important staging effects were also developed: the use of multiple stage sets, to reveal more than one physical locale at a time, and the appearance of the three-dimensional set, certainly a far cry from the painted backdrops that had lingered from the Restoration period. These new staging designs were lit by gas, until the appearance of electricity transformed the art of stage lighting forever.

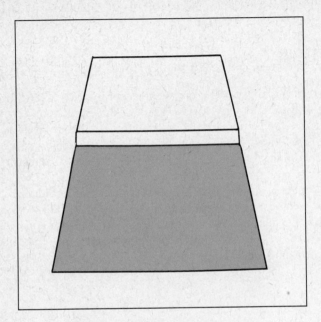

The elevated proscenium stage of the popular box set provides a sharp separation between actors and audience. (View from back of theatre.) Shaded area indicates the audience.

Melodrama and the Well-Made Play

In France two popular traditions of drama profoundly influenced the playwriting styles of the twentieth century. The first of these was *melodrama*, a term that in its broader context included the Romantic dramas of the late eighteenth and early nineteenth centuries but incorporated even later dramas, in which the ingredients of tragedy and comedy were deftly combined with elements of intrigue and disguise. For the first time ever, audiences applauded the valiant hero and his attempts to rescue the innocent heroine from the clutches of the villain.

The other major innovation was the *pièce bien faite*, translated as the "well-made play," invented by the French playwright Eugene Scribe (1791–1861). As a reaction against the formless extravagance of Romanticism, Scribe created a tightly structured, almost mechanical play format that was guaranteed to appeal to "typical" audience taste. Its "beginning-middle-end" design was deliberately contained within three carefully balanced acts, and its easily identifiable characters experienced some cliff-hanging situations that were usually—and predictably—worked out by the final-act curtain.

Stepping into the Twentieth Century

With our sharpened insight into stage history, let us enhance our perspective by constructing a model for twentieth-century drama. It is essential to establish at this point that "modern" becomes "contemporary" after the year 1945.

The modern playwright abandons the past. Whether through dramatic style (format of the play) or dramatic content (subject of the play), the modern playwright *avoids* associations with worn-out styles and themes. In style, Henrik Ibsen's *Doll's House* (1879) exemplifies the well-made play. Its subject matter and theme, however—that women are men's equals—qualifies as modern. This is demonstrated in a final stage action, when the protagonist, Nora Helmer, actually walks out on family and household, slamming the door behind her. When Ibsen wrote his play, events like this had never been so boldly portrayed on the stage.

In Eugene Ionesco's *Bald Soprano* (1950), two strangers, a man and woman, carry on a conversation in which they discover that they not only share the same house and sleep in the same bed but are indeed married to each other and have produced several children together. The absurd encounter is expressed through repetition, gibberish, and meaningless nonsequiturs, all of which contrast with playwriting styles of the past. Ionesco's innovative technique influenced a generation of contemporary European, British, and American playwrights, creating a tradition known as *Theatre of the Absurd*.

The modern playwright adheres to the "realistic" attitude. In portraying character and event, the modern playwright uses the drama *to show life as it is really lived*. *Realism* emerged during the latter half of the nineteenth century to accommodate those playwrights who wanted to tackle bolder themes and create characters whose dialogue and emotions were portrayed more naturally. In effect, they asked their audiences to imagine that an invisible *fourth wall* stood between them and the actors on stage. The concept would have lasting psychological repercussions on modern drama, allowing playwrights and actors to work with greater freedom, as if there were no audience present. Above all, the audience, in the role of voyeur, or "peeping Tom," looked through this imaginary wall to witness the behaviors of actors—as stage characters—who pretended to be unseen by their audience.

In modern realism, an especially unglamorous stage action often earns the unflattering label of *kitchen sink drama*. In the hands of a sensitive playwright, however, this realistic *slice of life*, as the technique is appropriately called, can be powerful indeed. Edward Albee's exploration of contemporary marriage in *Who's Afraid of Virginia Woolf?* (1962) seems uncannily real in its forthright and uninhibited language and in its candid depiction of the relationships of its four characters. Although it may not suit the taste of every playreader, Albee's need to explore the seamier sides of his characters' lives conforms with contemporary stage realism.

In *Miss Julie* (1888), August Strindberg established a variation of realism, also quite popular with modern dramatists, called *naturalism*. This style is more clinical in its detail and allows the playwright to detach himself from his characters and their behaviors, as if the forces of environment and heredity are determining each character's destiny. Thus, the fate that awaits the protagonist is worked out in a series of *seemingly* uncontrollable actions. As playreaders we know that Strindberg has contrived these actions. But in acknowledging the emotional upheavals that surround Miss Julie, we accept the inevitability of her tragic outcome.

The modern playwright emphasizes a Freudian interpretation of life. Although the eminent founder of psychoanalysis, Sigmund Freud (1856–1939), was greatly influenced by literature, especially the classical Greek dramas and the plays of Shakespeare, his own influence on contemporary literature was profound. The effect has been especially apparent in modern American drama, where the influence of Freudian theory, with its emphasis on sexual and psychological motivations, is apparent in many important plays. Eugene O'Neill, who originated a distinctly modern American drama, was profoundly influenced by Freudian theories. In *Desire under the Elms* (1924), his focus on a mother-son relationship—at once the salvation and destruction of its two protagonists—not only mirrored Freud's controversial Oedipal theory but also influenced a range of American playwrights who found powerful source material to investigate.

A summing up of all of the previous historical perspectives suggests that a good play:

1. *Satisfies the intellect.* It should concern a facet of human experience that is important and fresh; its topicality interests us.

2. *Shows organization.* In its observance of a particular form there should be economy, novelty, and impact, as well as balance between character and situation.

3. *Shows ideational content.* It should move our emotions; its characters and conflicts should grip us; certain aspects of the play must remain with us.

With our vertical perspective established, we are now prepared to populate our stages with living characters. But before doing so, let us glance briefly at some important horizontal perspectives, to develop a more universal view of drama.

Origins of African Drama

Approaching the horizontal perspective of the theatre requires a sharp turning away from our previous discussion, a healthy disassociation with historical chronology, rigid Aristotelian structures, and script-oriented performance styles. What we can borrow from our discussion are those concepts of *ritual* and *community.* These should help us establish a clear appreciation of the origins of African and Asian theatre and their relationship to Western tradition.

For black American artists, as well as their audiences, comfortably schooled in Aristotle, the spiritual journey *back* to Africa—to the dawn of civilization—has included a search for meaningful associations with their rich and exotic heritage. While the challenge of conjoining both cultures has proved disorienting to many black Americans, certain theatre practitioners have successfully adhered to the Western mold of drama—that is, those *popular* and *literary* forms—while preserving the classical elements of their native drama, which include *folk* and *primitive.*

Popular and Literary versus Folk and Primitive

Traditional African performances, which incorporated both primitive and folk traditions, fell into three styles, all of which employed music or a rhythmic drumbeat. The first was *ceremonial*, in which tribe members gathered on special occasions to socialize and participate in community rituals; the second was *storytelling*, where music and dance accompanied the narration and dialogue of elected participants; the third was *dance*, in which fragmentary elements of music and dialogue contributed to the communal tribal dances. In contrast with these, the conventional contemporary drama of Africa has embraced both popular and literary forms, partially influenced by Western models. Its most skilled playwrights have dealt with the controversial issues of a modern Africa, often mirroring the continent's political diversity.

The highly *codified* or structured rituals of traditional African performance, like the trope chanted centuries later upon the medieval church altar, were not intended to be artistic creations. On the contrary, they were entirely religious in nature. But the playreader will begin to see how an interpretation of ritual, given a degree of audience participation, costume elaboration, and arrangement of events, might easily be construed as dramatic performance. That is exactly how African ritual was transformed to the status of high theatrical art. The playreader will also see how the unstructured and improvisational nature of African performance departed radically from later Western traditions, which emphasized the clash of opposing forces and the exaltation of such conflict.

Influences of Music and Dance

For the contemporary Western audience acquainted with musical forms, *jazz* might serve as a significant link to our understanding of the traditional drama of Africa, where music has always played a vital role in ritual and theatrical performance. The seemingly spontaneous, improvisational style of jazz is capable of generating a range of moods and emotions in the listener. Whether subtly or wildly expressive, its intricate musical style is deceptively codified; its inbuilt rules create a bond between performer and audience that provides insight into the spirit of community that characterized tribal performance.

In turn, the influence of African tribal performance on dance, music, and drama in North America was considerable. When the first African slaves arrived in the sixteenth century, their extroverted community rituals could not be contained either on the slaveships or at the plantation huts. Being unacquainted with Western traditions in Europe and America, their unreserved native vitality, tribal impulses, and exotic rhythms naturally evolved into art forms, notably in music and dance, that quickly became integrated into the American culture. The African drum was replaced with bone clappers, hand clapping, and foot tapping. The foot tapping, in its imitation of the tribal drum beat, evolved into the popular *tap dance* in which two performers would tap out their conversation in much the same way the tribal drums communicated signals over long distances.

This dance tradition soon became an integral part of the nineteenth-century Negro *minstrel,* a legitimate and popular art form that incorporated the talents of prominent black artists and has demonstrated a strong impact on the contemporary American musical theatre. Minstrel performances, later performed by whites in "blackface," gradually developed into popular skits based on black characters and their life-styles, producing a negative stereotyping that would last for many decades. By the middle of the nineteenth century, the appearance of "social tracts"—those earliest dramas that echoed the polemics of the black journalist and statesman, Frederick Douglass—by the first black playwrights heralded the arrival of an indigenous black drama. Although these emerging dramas occasionally succumbed to stereotyping, they slowly repaired the damaged theatrical image of the black American.

Contemporary Black American Drama

As playreaders we must recognize that historians and critics of the black theatre in America—whether they are white or black—reflect important attitudes and perceptions in their writings on the subject. Prior to the revolutionary 1960s, the label "black" hardly existed to define those dark-skinned persons of African origins who populated the American theatre. The word *negro,* which gained pejorative associations in the 1970s, prevailed for many decades. The transformation of these labels has incorporated a transformed aesthetic as well. Forever relegated to the "negro period" are the often retold beginnings of the blacks in drama: the depiction in plays of English authorship, from the time of the American revolution, of the stereotyped "darkie" and buffoon who danced, joked, made uncouth remarks, and appeared docile, self-effacing, and always amusing; this was the consistent portrayal by white actors in blackface in both drama and minstrel.

Despite the achievements of black playwrights during the first half of the twentieth century, it was Lorraine Hansberry's *Raisin in the Sun* (1959) that served as an important turning point for contemporary black drama in America. For many white audiences, black theatre "began" with this enormously popular play. Having much in common with white domestic dramas, in both theme and structure, the play focused in its own subtle way on the clash between black and white. But with its south Chicago setting, its chauffeur hero, and its theme of the "dream deferred," this play was quickly elevated to the heights of protest drama in the timely early dawn of the civil rights movement in America. As a black play it reflected the concerns of the new "revolutionary" black playwrights.

In 1965 playwright Le Roi Jones demanded a theatre *about* black people, *with* black people, *for* black people and *only* black people, and the Black Power movement in microcosm was born. In contrast with its earlier "negro" counterpart, the Black Arts movement, of which Jones (Imamu Amiri Baraka) was the most vehement spokesman, was a radical alternative to the worn-out formulas of non-black playwrights. More recent trends have documented the American black artist's spiritual journey back to his African heritage to retrieve whatever influences might enhance his own style of dramatic performance. Although a very different set of political circumstances prevail on the African continent—for example, apartheid, which has generated powerful themes in dramatic literature—the increasing variety of such themes and performance styles sheds new light on the depth and vastness of the black drama.

As playreaders our investigation of twentieth-century black drama in America calls for the following considerations:

1. The popular domestic or family drama remains centrally important, often including a matriarchal figure who is pivotal to the play's characters and actions.

2. While issues of protest, including the clash between black and white, characterize many pre- and post-civil rights plays, black playwrights have become less preoccupied with these themes.

3. A search for African roots has revived authentic styles, seen in all areas of black performance but especially in the drama, where

a renewed literary interest in the continent's political diversity and turmoil has brought popular acclaim to native African playwrights like Wole Soyinka and Athol Fugard.

Asian Drama

A viable link between Asian drama and other world traditions will be found, yet again, in its origins of ritual and community. What the drama of Asia shares with African tradition, but not with its Western counterpart, is that *dance and theatre are essentially one and the same* and that *the drama does not conveniently conform to a chronological classification of styles.* The framework is further complicated by the range of religious doctrines of Buddhism, Confucianism, Islam, and Hinduism. This is further intensified by the cross-cultural connections of India, China, Japan, and Southeast Asia. While it is entirely possible that Eastern and Western traditions of drama have influenced each other during their mutual historical developments, the traditions vary so greatly that influences have been underplayed.

The documented drama of India began about the fifth century B.C., with performances designed primarily for the gods. The dramatic tradition dealt with universally shared and known myths, the same ones retold for centuries through a three-fold process of *improvisation, elaboration,* and *embellishment.* This process affects both dance and music modalities today, allowing the performers to go *beyond* the text, rather than being *bound* by the text. In the popular Kathakali dance theatre, for example, a performer might wish to express: "It's a beautiful night! Your eyes are beautiful! I love you!" Through improvisation, elaboration, and embellishment, however, the dancer might take up to forty-five minutes to establish the essential visual concepts of *beautiful night, eyes,* and *love.* Both performer and audience take delight in this embellishment, knowing fully what to expect in the performance. Plot development, climax, and denouement—those essential ingredients of the Western drama—simply do not exist. Instead the dance-drama establishes itself as *interpretive* and *reflexive* rather than *narrative* and *expressive.*

The literary epic sources for all themes in classical Indian drama are the *Ramayana* and the *Mahabharata,* two Hindu works that record the thoughts of many unknown poets. Another critical influence, although not a literary one, is the *Natyashastra,* compiled between 2 B.C. and 2 A.D. by anonymous collaborators, traditionally regarded to be divinely inspired. This *dramaturgical* work is encyclopedic in scope; it serves as a handbook for actors and incorporates every aspect of theatrical performance, including aesthetic principles, music interpretation, theatre architecture, and the meanings of the postures and hand gestures introduced by the actor in performance. Any comparison between this document and Aristotle's *Poetics* might seem superficial, at least in the light of their respective purposes, but their influences on the dramatic art of their individual cultures have proved considerable.

Between 250 B.C. and 1000 A.D., the literary tradition of Sanskrit drama dominated the courtly society of India. Some four hundred Sanskrit plays combined the ingredients of music, dance, spectacle, and ritual. The classical Sanskrit tradition was replaced in the tenth century by a popular folk drama that remains popular today. One form of this folk drama, known as the *Ramalila*, resembles the medieval cycles of England and Western Europe. These Rama and Krishna play cycles incorporate processional stagings, elaborate rituals, and the participation of mass audiences. Poetic speech, choreographed movements of actors, elaborate costuming and makeup—all of these elements contribute to the spectacle, which is still performed on special occasions.

Japanese Performance Styles

Our horizontal perspective of drama history closes with the theatrical traditions of Japan. Like the performance origins of other continents, the Japanese tradition emerged from a religious framework, incorporating the temple rituals and mythical tales of gods and men. The performance slowly separated from religious ritual, in much the same way that the liturgical play "went public" in medieval England.

A categorical consideration of Japanese theatre points to four styles: *Bugaku, Noh, Bunraku,* and *Kabuki. Bugaku,* which literally means "dance and music," has preserved these ancient arts in Japan. Kabuki, which was developed by a woman in the early seventeenth century, is now performed by male actors. Designed as an improvisational performance style, it has undergone continuous experimentation and modernization that even today shocks Kabuki traditionalists. Noh, established in the fourteenth century by two actors, Kanami and his son Zeami, unites the disparate traditions of dance, song, dialogue, farce, and magic, all within an unplotted structure. Significant for its use of masks, this theatrical tradition's 240 extant plays, intelligible only to those who are educated in Noh style, constitute a major contribution to early Japanese literature. Noh has had a circuitous impact on Western performance: the simplicity and economy of style, the central importance of the actor on an unadorned stage, and the directness of tone have influenced the work of certain contemporary directors trained in Western traditions.

Bunraku has enjoyed an even wider impact. Developed between the seventeenth and nineteenth centuries, these puppet performers, one-third human size, know no limitations as they seem to fly across the stage, exchange or alter heads, and perform magical feats. They are manipulated by one to three puppeteers who are disguised in black garments. Although puppet performance in Western culture has never achieved popularity as a mainstream theatrical style, the Asian tradition of masks and puppets has influenced the work of the Bread and Puppet Theatre, Mummenschanz, Julie Taymor, Ralph Lee, and Theodora Skipitares.

The occasional "easternization" of Western performance is further seen in the accumulative efforts of such artists as: British director Peter Brook, whose most ambitious performance piece, The Mahabharata (1986), has been inspired by the literary epic of India; American composer Philip Glass, whose improvisatory musical style shows the influence of the North Indian raga and whose opera Satyagraha (1980) is sung entirely in Sanskrit; and French choreographer Maurice Bejart, whose dance work Bhakti (1968) blends Hinduism and Western traditions. These efforts, among so many others, reflect the global reawakening that has characterized recent theatrical performance.

Themes for Analysis: Theatre History

As members of a technological society, we automatically contribute—as participants or observers—to the rituals of everyday life. The preceding historical framework strengthens our understanding of Western and non-Western perspectives and serves as backdrop for our own investigation.

1. Itemize your observations of a live sports (or theatre) performance. Show how the design of the stadium (or theatre) affected the performance and, more important, how it contributed to your enjoyment of the performance. (In approaching this discussion, suggested items worth noting might include the

dimensions of the performance space, spectator/performer relationships, performer/performer relationships, *general* lighting effects versus *specific* lighting effects, and acoustical impressions or sound effects.)

2. Identify the rituals of a live religious service—for example, the entrance/exit of the celebrants, the coordinated physical movements of the celebrants and the congregation, the use and handling of properties (props), the roles of music or singing. Discuss the theatrical (performance) values of these rituals, and show how they united the celebrants (performers) and congregation (audience). (Try to incorporate any insights gained from question 1 in your discussion.)

3. Consider the nonreligious practical rituals of everyday life: *political* (inaugural ceremonies), *civic* (parades, tree plantings), *military* (trouping the colors), *sociological* (teenage gang doings in black leather costumes, dancing in punk attire), *psychological* (the handshake). Identify and discuss the theatrical values of these practical rituals.

4. Briefly trace the development of theatre history (both Western and non-Western), identifying the similarities and contrasts between specific historical eras. (Try to facilitate your discussion by acknowledging the vertical and horizontal perspectives that connect these eras. For example: "Aspects of ritual and community, which characterize the dramas of ancient Greece and medieval England, are equally manifested in the classical dance theatre of India.")

5. In your reading of one twentieth-century play—for example, *Desire under the Elms* (O'Neill), *The Bald Soprano* (Ionesco), or *Who's Afraid of Virginia Woolf?* (Albee)—cite and discuss those elements of *style* and *content* that are considered "modern."

6. Rent the home video of Japanese film director Akira Kurosawa's *Throne of Blood* (inspired by Shakespeare's *Macbeth*) or James Ivory–Ismail Merchant's *Shakespeare Wallah*. In the Kurosawa film, observe the workings of the protagonist, the multiple scenes, and the denouement—all Western ingredients set against a Japanese landscape. Structure your observations into a short composition. In the Ivory/Merchant film, notice the striking cultural differences between the English acting company touring the provinces of India and the society for whom they perform. Incorporate these contrasts into a short composition.

7. Lorraine Hansberry's *Raisin In the Sun* (1959), LeRoi Jones's *Slave Ship: A Historical Pageant* (1967), and Athol Fugard's *Blood Knot* (1961) reflect the consciousness of three separate eras of contemporary black history. List your observations of these historical and dramaturgical differences. Contrast some of them with specific reference to each play.

CHAPTER TWO
THE PATTERNS AND DYNAMICS OF STAGE CHARACTERS

The world must be peopled!
—*Much Ado about Nothing*, II, iii

Shakespeare's rousing proclamation, spoken by a newly inspired Benedick, might well apply to the stage. Characters are so vital, they literally define the art of drama and distinguish it from all other literary genres. As playreaders we must visualize them in our mind's eye—a hearty challenge to our imagination that is facilitated by certain clues introduced by the playwright or suggested by the stage conventions of his time. But without his characters to articulate his ideas, the playwright stands defenseless. Therefore we can safely assume the following:

(1) *Characters contrast with each other.* In Shakespeare's *King Lear* (1607), two of Lear's daughters, Regan and Goneril, are heartless antagonists; a third, Cordelia, is genuinely good. The labels of protagonist and antagonist meaningfully denote their contrasting natures. Were it not for these differences, Lear's fate would be considerably altered, as would the outcome of the play. In Albee's *Zoo Story* (1959), Peter and Jerry share the same park bench, but while Peter is impeccably dressed, Jerry is disheveled. Their physical appearances initiate a set of contrasts central to the play's unexpected outcome.

(2) *Characters are either three-dimensional or one-dimensional, round or flat.* Bertolt Brecht's Mother Courage (1941) is an *eponymous* character, that is, the protagonist after whom the play is named. The playwright portrays her feelings and behavior realistically, allowing her to emerge as a three-dimensional, or round, character. In the same play, however, the Chaplain is one-dimensional: as one of her camp-followers, he is a "mouthpiece" who spouts a questionable morality and alters his clerical garb to accommodate whichever religious belief is safe to preach. Despite the necessary humor he brings to the play, his function is predictable and limited.

(3) *Characters are either central (pivotal) to the play's action or supportive (satellite), that is, circulating in the central character's orbit.* These designations flexibly apply to rank as well as *spatial relationships.* In Arthur Miller's *Death of a Salesman* (1949), Willie Loman's rank is pivotal to the play's actions and character relationships, since all other characters travel in his orbit and become supportive figures in his journey. Once having determined Loman's rank, we must consider his spatial relationship to the characters around him, more clearly facilitated if we visualize *Death of a Salesman* in the traditional box set, then populate this set with the play's characters. Most playwrights use professional stage terminology to designate the individual physical movements (i.e., *blocking*) of each character. Perhaps Willie Loman stands at stage center (the center of the performance space), then slowly moves *upstage* (toward the imaginary rear wall) or *downstage* (toward the audience, where the playreader observes the action) or circulates between *stage left* and *stage right* areas. On the basis of these essential movements, the playreader must imagine a physical strategy that mirrors the characters' motivated interactions. Let us visualize another example: Masha, Olga, and Irina, the protagonists of Anton Chekhov's *Three Sisters* (1901), become physically highlighted, contrasted, and ultimately isolated in relation to the many satellite characters who invade their individual and collective worlds. Their unique triangular relationship suggests a small chorus positioned against the play's larger chorus of characters.

(4) *Characters inspire audience identification.* Although we are intrigued by sudden plot twists and provoked by gripping themes, stage characters incorporate our immediate responses by appealing to our own humanity. Nevertheless, we must avoid psychoanalyzing them as if they are real people. To equate any fictional portrait with a human counterpart is psychologically unsound, as the two are rarely compatible. For example, we neither condone nor condemn Euripides's Medea for her revenge on Jason in the slaughtering of their two sons. Instead we recognize Medea's *identity* as a woman scorned. We should try to think less in terms of *character* than *identity*, as character denotes *limitation*, while identity implies *wholeness*.

(5) *Characters are universal and constant.* Although it may be psychologically unsound to equate our lives with fictional stage characters, we may draw some important conclusions about our own human natures in relation to the characters we view on the stage or printed page. Familiarity with a variety of character portraits ultimately

breeds a certain recognition, until we perceive some continuity from one generation of character types to another. The tragedy of war affects Euripides's Hecuba in *The Trojan Women* (415 B.C.) in much the same way that it disorients Pavlo Hummel's mother in David Rabe's *Basic Training of Pavlo Hummel* (1971). A mother's loss is universal, as seen when more than two thousand years separate the respective playwrights. Lear's anger toward his ungrateful children is echoed by Willy Loman centuries later in Miller's *Death of a Salesman*. We can connect stage characters to each other using the bonds common to humanity.

The following classification of general character types, stage conventions, and effects should help us identify the major patterns, relationships, and distinguishing qualities among characters who "people" the drama:

Classical Greek Drama

Character types
— Kings, Queens, Chorus, Nurse, Messenger
— Prototypes who set examples
— Limited supporting cast

Stage conventions
— Male actors wearing tragic masks
— Verse dialogue, monologue format
— Exaggerated voices and gestures
— Daylight performance

Effect: Despite one-dimensional prototypes, audiences are stirred by legendary themes, heroic characters, and head-on confrontations.

Dynamics of Character Relationships
Character case study: *Oedipus Rex* (Sophocles, 426 B.C.)
Protagonist: Oedipus, king of Thebes, married to Jocasta
Personality type: Proud, head-strong
Antagonist: Creon, brother of Jocasta

Conflict: Defendant unknowingly murders his father, King Laius, then marries his mother, Jocasta; he decides to uncover the truth of his origin. As his quest deepens, so does his conflict with Creon.

Outcome: Defendant blinds self, then goes into exile. Creon assumes crown.

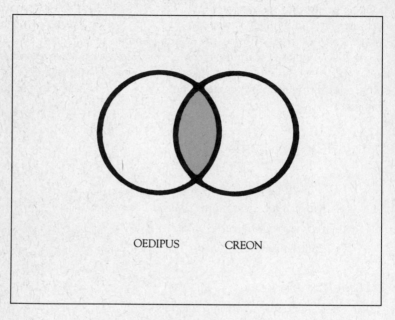

OEDIPUS   CREON

Direct, confrontational conflict between character prototypes.

Character Commentary

In the contemporary theatre, *character continuity* retains the function of Chorus, as narrator and conscience for the protagonist, to be performed by characters like Tom Wingfield in Tennessee Williams's *Glass Menagerie* (1945) or the Stage Manager in Thornton Wilder's *Our Town* (1938). The function of Messenger is performed by one-dimensional "mouthpieces" who bear news that affects the play's outcome: for example, Leo Hubbard in Lillian Hellman's *Little Foxes* (1939). Even the supporting character of the Nurse—Medea's loyal confidante and companion in Euripides's play—inspires a tradition of familiar types: Juliet's Nurse in Shakespeare's *Romeo and Juliet* (1595);

the outspoken maid, Dorine, in Moliere's *Tartuffe* (1669); and Miss Prism, the governess in Oscar Wilde's *Importance of Being Earnest* (1895).

Classical Roman Comedy

Character Types
—Mischievous twins (mistaken identities)
—Designing courtesans
—Lovelorn suitors
—Stubborn old men
—Braggart soldiers
—Cunning servants
—Parasites
—Transvestites (cross-dressers)

Stage Conventions
—Male actors wearing comic masks
—Verse dialogue combined with colloquial speech
—Extended jokes, song interludes, and sight gags
—Daylight performance
Effect: Stock characters supply the lowbrow Roman audience with endless bellylaughs, appealing to their decadent tastes.

Roman Comedy and the *Commedia Dell'arte*

There can be little doubt that the stock figures of the *commedia dell'arte*, a famous improvisational theatre that flourished in Italy from the sixteenth through the eighteenth centuries, were inspired by the characters of Plautus and Terence. No complete playscripts exist as the performers improvised their dialogue. Such familiar characters as the cunning servant, Arlecchino (Harlequin); the tricked husband or

*Wide Sampling of the Tradition and Influence
of Roman Comic Characters*

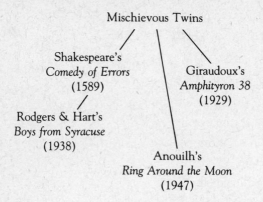

Mischievous Twins

Shakespeare's
Comedy of Errors
(1589)

Giraudoux's
Amphityron 38
(1929)

Rodgers & Hart's
Boys from Syracuse
(1938)

Anouilh's
Ring Around the Moon
(1947)

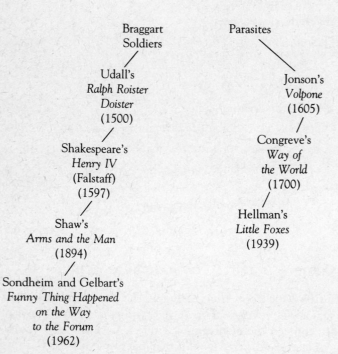

Braggart
Soldiers

Parasites

Udall's
*Ralph Roister
Doister*
(1500)

Jonson's
Volpone
(1605)

Shakespeare's
Henry IV
(Falstaff)
(1597)

Congreve's
*Way of
the World*
(1700)

Shaw's
Arms and the Man
(1894)

Hellman's
Little Foxes
(1939)

Sondheim and Gelbart's
*Funny Thing Happened
on the Way
to the Forum*
(1962)

stubborn father, Pantalone; the braggart Captain; and Columbina, the clever maid, are all sharply reminiscent of their classical Roman counterparts. Finally, we recognize their distinctive characteristics in modern stage figures; the innocent young lovers of the *commedia* evolved into the dashing "romantic lead" and "pretty ingenue," as we popularly typecast them today. Rare is the play that exists without one or several such characters influenced by the Italian *commedia*.

Character Commentary

Stage and society have mirrored each other for centuries, beginning with the classical drama, in which a certain fascination for exchanging gender identities enabled men to portray women characters. This professional phenomenon has instigated other related performance issues that have continued into the present. Elements of transvestitism, popularly known as "drag" or cross-dressing, in which the stage character assumes the guise of the opposite sex as an integral part of the story line, were fostered in the low comic antics of classical Roman comedy. The stage convention proved popular in the plays of Shakespeare, where male actors portrayed female characters who, in the course of the action, must cross-dress as men for "survival"—an element of the play's theme that is carefully integrated with its plot: Rosalind in *As You Like It* (1599) or Viola in *Twelfth Night* (1601). The transformation was a type of "double-cross." In modern theatre, the phenomenon is continually manifested in both serious and comic plays: Barnaby Tucker's female disguise—strictly for story development—in Thornton Wilder's *Matchmaker* (1954); Contessa Geschwitz's male attire—a reference to her lesbian attraction to Lulu—in Franz Wedekind's tragedy, *Earth Spirit* (1894); and Arnold's "drag" getup—one aspect of the character's development—in the first part of Harvey Fierstein's *Torch Song Trilogy* (1982). If, as Hamlet exclaims, actors "are the abstract and brief chronicles of the time," their stage characters often reflect contemporary society's preoccupation with cosmetic "gender shifts" or with *androgyny*, in which the integration of both masculine and feminine characteristics transcends a specific gender classification.

Medieval Drama

Character Types
—Old and New Testament figures
—Personifications of virtues and vices
—The appearance of "Everyman"

Stage Conventions
—Verse dialogue
—Use of male and some female performers
—Play-cycle format
Effect: Flat, one-dimensional characters, limited to stilted religious dialogue, prove popular with audiences who are taught moral lessons while they are entertained.

(1500)

EVERYMAN

FAUST

HAMLET

LEAR

PEER GYNT

MR. ANTROBUS

WILLY LOMAN

(1949)

Character Commentary

The characters of the medieval drama are dominated by the figure of Everyman, the protagonist of the medieval morality play or allegory of the same title, whose author is unknown. Everyman's life journey brings him in contact with virtues and vices, personified as stage characters. The appearance of Everyman influences the development of subsequent stage characters whose universal experiences also mirror humanity. Notable classical examples are Marlowe's Doctor Faustus (1592) and Shakespeare's Hamlet and Lear. More modern characters include Ibsen's eponymous Peer Gynt (1857), George Antrobus in Wilder's Skin of Our Teeth (1942), and Willy Loman in Miller's Death of a Salesman (1949).

Not coincidentally, the name of Miller's protagonist, Willy Loman, aptly points to his common or low-man (Loman) character ancestry.

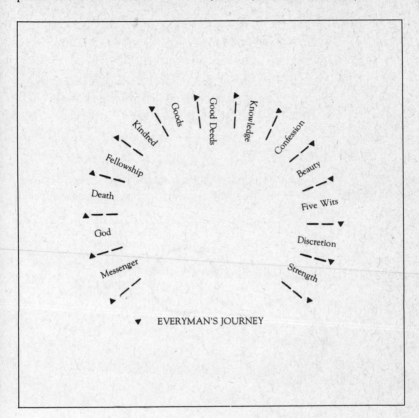

Elizabethan Drama

Character Types
— Royalty, noble and heroic types
— Supporting cast of upper-class types
— Clowns, mechanicals
— Mixture of round and flat characters
— Sharply contrasted character traits

Stage Conventions

—Verse-dialogue
—Monologue format
—Male actors, no masks
—Daylight performances

Effect: Intricate psychological motivations, multiple settings, and complex character relationships fascinate audiences from all levels of society.

Character Commentary

Shakespeare's world is filled with characters who display detailed, realistic traits easily recognized by the contemporary playreader. We are

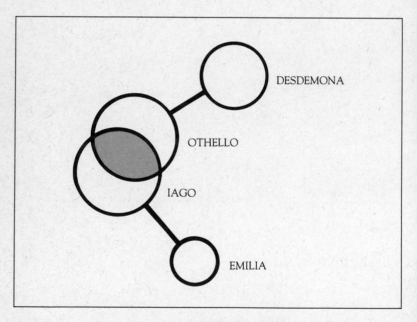

While the central eponymous character, Othello (protagonist), shares the spotlight with Iago (antagonist), the chain reaction instigated by Iago affects numerous satellite characters, including their respective spouses.

especially fascinated by those characters who remain innately connected to their darker sides or purposes. In our consideration of character continuity, Elizabethan stage character components reflect medieval personifications as well. The universality of Hamlet, the generosity of Portia, and the innocence of Desdemona share the same stage with the vices of Edmund and Iago. Because of their complexity and indispensable function as antagonists, we are immediately susceptible to the challenges and contrasts Edmund and Iago offer their protagonists.

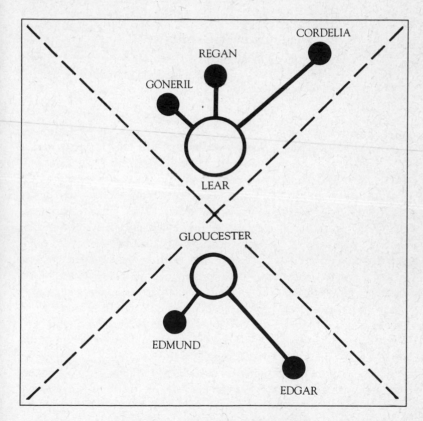

We observe a certain symmetry or balance in the character relationships of *King Lear:* the "Lear versus daughters" dynamic is mirrored by the "Gloucester versus sons" dynamic.

Restoration and Eighteenth-Century Drama

Character Types

—Amoral, acid-tongued sophisticated ladies and gentlemen

—One-dimensional and three-dimensional fops, schemers, gossips, and flirts

Stage Conventions

—Prose dialogue for comedies; verse for tragedies

—Male and female actors

—Establishment of the indoor box set

Effect: Elitist court audience enjoys seeing its petty intrigues mirrored by a collection of colorful, often underhanded characters.

Character Commentary

It would be no exaggeration to claim that this brood of Restoration and eighteenth-century characters, including Horner, Valentine, Fainall, Lady Wishfort, Tony Lumpkin, and Mrs. Malaprop are the stylish forerunners of the popular comedy-of-manners stage characters of the nineteenth and twentieth centuries. Quick to bed rather than wed, many of these artificially mannered and elaborately costumed dames, damsels, and dandies are surrounded by satellite characters who often serve as mouthpieces—a role equated with the messenger's in the classical drama—and swiftly perform whatever services will abet their masters and mistresses. Of course, no small credit belongs to Shakespeare, who devised the prototypical character match between Beatrice and Benedick in *Much Ado about Nothing* (1599), thereby establishing a tradition of "lovers" whose brand of flirtation, verbal dueling, and intellectual comedy continues to delight us.

A genealogy of those highly verbal and exceedingly witty characters who follow in Beatrice and Benedick's indelible footsteps would surely include: Congreve's Millamant and Mirabell, who seem perfectly at home verbalizing their own unique marital contract before committing themselves to each other; Sheridan's resilient Lady Teazle and Joseph Surface, whose relationship is a perfect reflection of the names they bear; Wilde's Gwendolen and Jack, whose brand of verbal artificiality triumphs hilariously over its vacuous content; Shaw's Ann Whitefield and Jack Tanner, who rail vociferously before yielding to the inevitable; Coward's Amanda and Elyot, who revive the elegance, amorality, and crackling wit of the Restoration period but make it seem curiously appropriate in their own modern surroundings; and not the least of all, Stoppard's Annie and Henry, whose attraction to each other is complicated by their modish charades in a contemporary society where true love or "the real thing" seems impossible to find.

Realistic Drama of the Late Nineteenth and Early Twentieth Centuries

Character Types
—Working class protagonists
—Mixture of round and flat characters
—Highly introspective character behaviors

Stage Conventions
—Prose dialogue appropriate for the new stage realism

Effect: Audiences readily identify with stage characters who express ideas and emotions without recourse to artificial verbal embellishment, archaic monologues, or exaggerated acting styles.

Character Commentary

What choices confront us when we explore the range of stage characters from the literature we classify as "modern"? In view of a certain "character continuity," how divorced are these modern characters from the boldly depicted character traits we confronted in Shakespeare but lost sight of during the Restoration drama? Allowing for some variation and embellishment, it is conceivable that Ibsen's three-dimensional, eponymous portrait of Hedda in *Hedda Gabler* (1890) is the embodiment of jealousy and evil yet remains a startling creation tempered by the emotional instability that has fashioned her life. Shaw allows Mrs. Warren in *Mrs. Warren's Profession* (1902) to embrace ambition yet never loses our sympathy for her. Blanche DuBois's spiritual beauty, which is no match for Stanley Kowalski's brutality, survives triumphantly in Williams's *Streetcar Named Desire* (1947). Robert Bolt's Sir Thomas More, in *A Man for All Seasons* (1961), personifies reason and patience but is

GENEALOGY OF CHARACTERS
OF THE
COMEDY OF MANNERS

Beatrice & Benedick

Much Ado about Nothing (1599)
William Shakespeare

Millamant & Mirabell

The Way of the World (1700)
William Congreve

Lady Teazle & Joseph Surface

The School for Scandal (1777)
Richard Brinsley Sheridan

Gwendolen & Jack

The Importance of Being Earnest (1895)
Oscar Wilde

Ann & Jack

Man and Superman (1903)
Bernard Shaw

Amanda & Elyot

Private Lives (1930)
Noel Coward

Annie & Henry

The Real Thing (1983)
Tom Stoppard

no less powerful in his political and religious convictions. The innocence of Pavlo Hummel, although not enough to save his life, is no less admirable in a country at war, in Rabe's *Basic Training of Pavlo Hummel*.

Theatre Companies versus Stage Characters

Two powerful forces influenced the dynamics of modern stage characters toward the end of the nineteenth century. The first was the advent of major international theatre companies, such as the Theatre Libre in France (1887), the Freie Buhne in Germany (1889), the Independent Theatre in London (1891), the Moscow Art Theatre (1897), the Abbey Theatre of Dublin (1903), and The Group Theatre in America (1931). All of these theatres encouraged the playwrights who wrote for them to create realistic characters tailored to the individual talents of each company's actors. The second force was the considerable control given to the innovative stage directors of these companies. In the Moscow Art Theatre, for example, it would be difficult to imagine the creation of Chekhov's vivid stage characters *without* the guidance of the theatre's co-founder and director, Constantin Stanislavsky. Chekhov's approach to stage characters, summarized in the following tendencies, became an indelible trademark:

1. Characters respond to the pauses or "silences" *between* the dramatic outbursts.

2. Characters show delicate nuances that build solidly and subtly.

3. Characters, both pivotal and supportive, have priority over plot.

4. Characters' emotional or interior lives are carefully played against each other in a prose dialogue that achieves a poetic lyricism.

The Chekhov-Stanislavsky impact proved so popular that the word *Chekhovian* soon referred to non-Chekhov characters and acting styles inspired by this new stage realism. Similar moody, introspective, soft-spoken but always emotion-charged characters populated the plays of writers who deliberately paid homage to Chekhov. They included Bernard Shaw, Lillian Hellman, Tennessee Williams, and Harold Pinter among many others. Foremost was American playwright Clifford Odets, who soon became the heralded working-class poet-playwright for the influential Group Theatre, whose directors, Lee Strasberg and Harold Clurman, supported Stanislavsky's theories. Odets created a variety of popular, if somewhat stereotypical, working-class protagonists who reflected the ideals of a much troubled, economically depressed American society.

In Chekhov's *Three Sisters*, Masha, Olga, and Irina are highlighted by the dozen characters who surround them. The relationships shared by both central and supportive characters in this play determine the strategies of dramatic action and alter the traditional view of character conflict.

Realistic Drama of the Mid-Twentieth Century

By the middle of the twentieth century, the modern stage character was replaced by a contemporary one: a working-class protagonist who has evolved into a nonconforming, antisocial, and relentlessly outspoken character. Influenced by the political and societal unrest around him, British playwright John Osborne turned Jimmy Porter—the "angry young man" of *Look Back in Anger* (1956)—into a fashionable antihero. Osborne's work, as well as that of his playwright contemporaries, also incorporates the more externalized character types from the work of German playwright Bertolt Brecht.

Character Types
—Working-class protagonists, outsiders, and anti-heroes
—Character behaviors externalized to accommodate a didactic realism

Stage Conventions
—Prose dialogue that still works for the new stage realism
—With Brecht's influence, song interludes that facilitate play's message

Effect: Despite his insulting, confrontational manner, the "angry young man" (or woman) wins the sympathy of his audience; his victimization seems directly related to sociopolitical problems also shared by the spectator. The "anti" or nontraditional hero suddenly achieves an authoritative "voice" on the popular stage.

At this point, the word *voice* becomes an essential component in our study, as we shift our attention from character patterns and dynamics to character "sounds," namely, those that express vocally the internal natures of the characters. Before doing so, let us consider how stage characters offer us a wide opportunity for literary discussion and analysis, especially in the areas of their functions, contrasts, and continuity.

Themes for Analysis: Characters

In contrast with the wider perspectives we encountered in our analyses of theatre history, a discussion of stage characters requires narrower considerations. Perhaps the most popular and challenging assignment is the *individual character sketch*. This focuses on a personal facet of the character or some striking theatrical purpose he or she serves in the play. With specific reference to the dialogue and actions of a selected stage character, and always mindful of what certain characters reveal about each other, our analyses will grow in depth and interest. The following topical statements, concentrating on the innumerable *functions* of stage characters, should set the tone for others as well:

1. "Brecht's Mother Courage: War Victim or War Profiteer."

2. "Mary Tyrone as Central Protagonist in O'Neill's *Long Day's Journey into Night.*"

3. "The Versatile Function of the Stage Manager in Wilder's *Our Town.*"

4. "Alan Strang's 'Hide-and-Seek' Behavior in Shaffer's *Equus.*"

5. "Durang's Sister Mary Ignatius: Character as Caricature."

6. "Bottom as Clown Figure in Shakespeare's *Midsummer Night's Dream.*"

7. "Willy Loman: Tragic Hero or Pathetic Victim in Miller's *Death of a Salesman.*"

8. "Lena Younger: The Voice of Reason in Hansberry's *Raisin in the Sun.*"

As stage characters frequently interact, the following pairs of characters serve as striking contrasts and reveal much about their relationships in the plays they inhabit. Incorporate these pairs, or others you might encounter in your playreading, into specific play-related themes:

1. "Antigone versus Creon: The Right to Dissent in Sophocles's Tragedy."

2. "Professor Higgins versus Mr. Doolittle: Portraits of the Social Classes in Shaw's *Pygmalion.*"

3. "Blanche Dubois versus Stanley Kowalski: Struggle and Survival in Williams's *Streetcar Named Desire.*"

4. "Ephraim versus Eben: Like Father, Unlike Son in O'Neill's *Desire under the Elms.*"

5. "Hecuba versus Helen: Human Casualties in Euripides's *Trojan Women.*"

6. "Edmund versus Edgar: Brothers 'Disunited' in Shakespeare's *King Lear.*"

7. "Petruchio versus Katharine: Chauvinistic Behaviors in Shakespeare's *Taming of the Shrew.*"

8. "Martha versus George: Self-Destructive Games in Albee's *Who's Afraid of Virginia Woolf?.*"

Mindful of the importance of theatre history and the various historical traditions from which stage characters emerge, we can appreciate more fully the significance of character continuity in the drama. Study the following themes carefully, and respond to them in brief verbal discussion or written composition. More important, use them as models to develop some of your own themes of character continuity, based on interesting characters you have met in your reading:

1. "How Plautus's Menaechmi Twins Are Reborn in Shakespeare's *Comedy of Errors.*"

2. "Medea's Nurse Meets Juliet's: A Study of Character Contrast and Continuity."

3. "Aspects of 'Everyman' in Modern Stage Characters."

4. "The Eternal Return of the Braggart Soldier in Drama."

5. "What Characters from the Comedy of Manners Have in Common with Each Other."

6. "Osborne's 'Angry Young Man' Meets His Classical Counterpart."

7. "Tracing the Working-Class Protagonist Back to His Noble Ancestry."

8. "Issues of Gender as Reflected in the Transformations of Selected Stage Characters."

CHAPTER THREE
HEARING CHARACTERS
COME ALIVE

Speak the speech, I pray you, as I pronounced
it to you trippingly on the tongue.
—*Hamlet*, III, ii

Hamlet's command to the players contains excellent advice for every playreader: *Speak the dialogue of the play aloud in order to make the characters come alive.* It is the voice within us that imaginatively transforms a literary character whose reality might otherwise seem hopelessly confined to the page. Allowing the playreader to "sound the character out," dialogue conveys important clues, motivates the character's external responses, and most of all, provides immediate access to his soul. Since character descriptions are often scant in what they tell us about each character's distinctive sound, many playwrights prefer to let the characters speak for themselves. Others may offer slight clues. Willy Loman is "past sixty years of age, dressed quietly." Does this imply that he "speaks" quietly? Nora Helmer simply enters the action without further comment from Ibsen. We must listen to her dialogue in order to assess her vocal dimensions. Does Lady Sneerwell's name reveal anything about her character or speech habits? When Lear says of Cordelia, "Her voice was ever soft / Gentle and low, an excellent thing in a woman," he provides us with a precious clue to a unique vocal personality that should contrast with Goneril's or Regan's. We can further appreciate why an actor's interpretation of a particular stage role will often affect the way we remember the character thereafter. Allowing us to hear the character's speech, the actor performs a vital task. As resourceful playreaders, however, we assume the actor's responsibility completely and discover for ourselves how to bring the playwright's characters to life.

What to Listen For

Whether it appears as words hastily strung together, eloquent verse, unaffected conversation, or garbled monosyllables, dialogue enhances our aural imagination in response to each stage character. Before significant character-dialogue relationships can be established, however, four vital acoustical components must be identified: *articulation, timbre, regionalism,* and *pace.* Since the art of speech is a dynamic process that incorporates these components simultaneously, the stage character becomes the embodiment of this dynamism.

Articulation

In Shakespeare's *King Lear,* Edmund's initial appearance and dialogue provide us with clues to his character, triggering a series of actions that affect the course of the play. Edmund has just learned of his legitimate brother Edgar's inheritance. The classical convention of the *soliloquy* allows Edmund to reveal his thoughts alone and aloud:

> Thou, Nature, art my goddess, to thy law
> My services are *bound.* Wherefore should I
> Stand in the plague of custom, and permit
> The curiosity of nations to deprive me,
> For that I am some twelve or fourteen moonshines
> Lag of a *brother?* Why *bastard?* Wherefore *base?*
> When my dimensions are as well compact,
> My mind as generous and my shape as true,
> As honest madam's issue? Why **brand** they us
>
> With **báse?** With **báseness? Bástardy? Báse, báse?**

It seems that Edmund's illegitimacy is going to cost him his fortune. But this message, which we can extract from the lines, takes second place next to the character's manner of pronouncing it. Thus *articulation* becomes the essential key to Edmund's character. The alliterative and repetitive uses of the *b* words cited above (italics and boldface are mine) contribute to Edmund's explosive and demonic nature. This voiced-plosive consonant—sounded as two lips sharply contract and release air—demands a facial distortion that complements the character's physical brutality and spiritual ugliness. Shakespeare understood the effect of this consonant's reverberation: the louder, harsher, more explosive Edmund's vocal attack, the more convincing his villainy. We hear Edmund's forthright, realistic tone powerfully sustained in the metrical verse pattern of *iambic pentameter,* emphasized in the five "beats" of the last line. Its succinct conversational intensity, much like a musical crescendo, captures the character's devouring need for recognition and power in a society that scorns his birthright.

There is an assortment of stage characters who depend on this more elaborate articulation to become actualized and, in turn, connect with the imaginary universes depicted in their plays. These vocal mannerisms, which constitute their strongest appeal as characters, also confirm their existences. One extreme and contemporary example is Lucky in Samuel Beckett's *Waiting for Godot* (1952), whose garbled, inarticulate pronunciation of key words and images lends special dimension to his character. The following uninterrupted flow of words characterizes his unique style:

> . . . that man in Possy of Testew and Cunard that man in Essy that man in short that man in brief in spite of the strides of alimentation and defecation wastes and pines wastes and pines and concurrently simultaneously what is more for reasons unknown in spite of the strides of physical culture the practice of sports such as tennis football running cycling swimming flying floating riding gliding conating camogie skating tennis of all kinds dying flying sports of all sorts. . . .

It is conceivable that Lucky's one opportunity for self-expression in the entire play—articulated here in this brief fragment from a lengthy monologue that is built on a single run-on sentence—might be appropriately highlighted by belching, choking, and stuttering speech behaviors. Beckett's dialogue is spoken by no ordinary character but rather by one whose neck happens to be tied to a rope or noose. For Lucky, who is so ironically named, articulation becomes a virtual act of survival.

A different kind of articulation is demonstrated by Richard Roma in David Mamet's *Glengarry Glen Ross* (1983). His violent nature thrives on a vernacular, carefully reinforced by a vocal precision that sets him apart from his clientele. Toward the play's conclusion, he shouts the following to a colleague:

> *Forget* the deal, Jimmy. [*Pause.*] *Forget* the deal . . . you know me. The deal's *dead.* Am I talking about the *deal?* That's *over.* Please. Let's talk about *you.* Come on . . . Come on. [*Pause.*] Come on, Jim. [*Pause.*] I want to tell you something. Your life is your own. You have a contract with your wife. You have certain things you do *jointly,* you have a *bond* then . . . and there are

other things. Those things are yours. You needn't feel *ashamed,* you needn't feel that you're being *untrue . . .* or that she would abandon you if she knew. This is your life. [*Pause.*] *Yes.* Now I want to *talk* to you because you're obviously upset and that *concerns* me. Now let's go. Right now.

Roma's double-talking, double-crossing manner is carefully conveyed through the calculated articulation of a highly selective vocabulary, of which fourteen key words—clearly italicized by the playwright—demand vocal emphasis, or punch. In short, his manner of speech weighs in as important as his message, the outcome of which crudely juxtaposes bedroom and business behaviors, and suggests, almost graphically, his lopsided code of professional ethics.

Timbre

Just as articulation reinforces the striking *oral* components of a character's sound, *timbre* embodies the character's *emotional* life. Once we have established the sounds of the character, it becomes important to *hear how the character feels.* How shall we determine the feelings of the following protagonist, a woman, whose first lines contain specific images central to her predicament?

Úp frŏm tħe ground—Ŏ weāry heád, Ŏ breāking néck.

Thís iš nŏ longer Tróy. Aňd wé aře nót →

    tħe lofds ŏf Tróy. ↘

Ĕndure. ↘ Tħe wáys ŏf fáte aře tħe wáys ŏf tħe wiňd. ↘

Dríft wĭth tħe stream—dríft wĭth fāte.

Nŏ uše tŏ túrn tħe próv tŏ bréast the wāves.

Lét tħe bŏat gó aš ĭt cháncĕs

Sorroẅ, mỹ sorrŏw.

Whát sórrŏw iš tħere tħat ís nŏt miñe, ↗

    gríef tŏ wéep fŏr. ↘

Coúntřy lóst aňd cħildrĕn aňd húsbănd.

Glorỹ ŏf áll mỹ hoúse broúght low.

Aĺl wăs nóthiňg—nóthiňg, álwaỹs. ↘

The speaker is Hecuba, the old queen of fallen Troy, in Euripides's *Trojan Women*. Edith Hamilton's effective verse translation retains a loose style that sacrifices none of the protagonist's urgency. This arrangement of poetic lines, known as *versification*, tangles with our eyes, imploring us to hear the vocal possibilities of Hecuba, whose feelings must convey, in a few short breaths, unfathomable horror, near-fatal fatigue, and a resignation to great personal loss. Exactly how does the playreader *hear* such range and depth of emotional expression? How will *timbre* be manifested?

Hecuba directs herself to lift her prostrate body off the ground and behold the bloody carnage that surrounds her. We must hear this first poetic line, and then envision it, in three separate movements: the slow physical turn and lift, the doubly sighed long O—"Oooo weary head, Oooo breaking neck"—twisted into a pronounced moan as her aged head on its aching neck confronts a sight that is no longer Troy. Her experience does not deceive her as she recollects that her rule as one of the "lords of Troy" has ended.

To hear Hecuba and sense her emotional responses is to abandon the pace of conversational speech. Or how else can Hecuba's next line, translated as a single command—"Endure!"—convey her acceptance of this reality? Do we imagine this command pronounced as a bloodcurdling rasp? Perhaps it is sounded in a long full-throated wail, "enduring" like its message. The next four lines allow her voice to sail with the rhythm of the verse, like a boat driven by the waves, until she is hurled into sorrow for country, children, and husband, all lost. But the sorrow, which is echoed two more times, must be resounded for impact and meaning. We imagine Hecuba weeping uncontrollably as she utters these final lines, testing the limits of her grief through a timbre that reflects the urgency of Euripides's "pacifist" theme.

Andrey's lengthy interrogatives, addressed to an old caretaker in Chekhov's *Three Sisters*, reflect a quieter desperation:

> Oh, where is it, ‖ where has it all gone, ‖ my past
> when I was <u>young</u>, <u>gay</u>, <u>clever</u>, when I dreamed and thought
> with grace, when my present and my future were <u>lighted up</u>
> <u>with hope</u>? Why is it that when we have barely begun to live,
> we grow <u>dull</u>, <u>gray</u>, <u>uninteresting, lazy</u>, <u>indifferent</u>, <u>useless</u>,
> <u>unhappy</u>?

His eloquent "interrogatives" echo an important theme: that the past is irretrievable. Key words like "young," "gay," "clever," or the image of a life "lighted up with hope" must be delicately sounded in our aural imagination, in order to contrast with the present and more painful reality of Andrey's life, reflected in a string of harshly struck adjectives like "dull," "gray," "useless," and "unhappy." Notice how the graceful balance of these two lines, translated from the Russian, retains a power and simplicity so essential to the *sound* of this character's longing or of questions that must go unanswered.

Regionalism

Realistic stage characters mirror their origins and their social status through the words they are given to speak. Here the sensitive playwright must carefully consider how his characters will be revealed to us. To assess the *regionalism* of a given character, for example, we should explore stage dialogue with the same freedom granted to the actor. Just as a confident director allows the actor, assisted by the playwright's words, extensive range to discover his character, so must we reconstruct a character whose regionalism bequeaths on him a certain identity or membership.

It is possible to appreciate the dialogue in Wilde's *Importance of Being Earnest* strictly for its uses of regionality. Not a word is spoken or an idea completed without our wanting to assess the speaker's background, status, or even education. Indeed, Wilde makes all of these elements accessible through the speech patterns of his characters. In the following scene, listen to the effect of Jack Worthing's sudden "proposal" to Gwendolen Fairfax and how it triggers her more calculated response: (Capitalization, used for emphasis, is mine.)

> J: Well . . . may I PROPOSE to you NOW?
>
> G: I think it would be an ADMIRABLE OPPORTUNITY. And to SPARE you any possible DISAPPOINTMENT, Mr. WORTHING, I think it only FAIR to tell you quite frankly BEFOREHAND that I am FULLY DETERMINED to ACCEPT you.
>
> J: GWENDOLEN!
>
> G: YES, Mr. WORTHING, WHAT have you got to say to me?
>
> J: You KNOW what I have got to say to you.
>
> G: YES, but you DON'T SAY it.

J: GWENDOLEN, will you MARRY ME? [*Goes on his knees.*]

G: Of COURSE I will, DARLING. How LONG you have
been about it! I am AFRAID you have had very LITTLE
EXPERIENCE in HOW to PROPOSE.

Although we assume that Jack and Gwendolen travel in a highly
civilized circle and should be "sounded" as cultivated, upper-crust
English types, we must also hear how their styles differ from each other.
Jack's impetuous yet halting manner is contrasted with Gwendolen's
cool, sophisticated assurance. She intuitively knows of his wish to
propose and even forewarns him of her acceptance. But the ritual must
be played out in carefully selected and articulated words: Jack's
swoonlike, heartfelt "Gwendolen, will you marry me?" is immediately
counteracted by her worldly acceptance and a pointed reprimand for his
lack of experience with marriage proposals.

Like the other characters in this play, Gwendolen and Jack seem
incapable of "conventional" intonations (the manner of producing
tones with regard to rise and fall in pitch). *Affectation*—a purposely
exaggerated speech behavior—is befitting to the social class Wilde
satirizes. Another possible formula for their popularity as stage characters is found in the playwright's permitting them to listen to and take
delight in every egocentric inch of their regionalism. Such vocal
affectations comment on the characters themselves and serve to
"accentuate" their insipidly delightful chatter.

The dynamics of regionalism shift radically in Williams's *Streetcar
Named Desire*, where several sharply drawn characters have as much to
discover about their respective vocal mannerisms as we do. Blanche
DuBois pays an extended visit to her sister Stella and meets, for the first
time, Stella's husband, Stanley. In the tight quarters of their New
Orleans flat the day after her arrival, Blanche asks Stanley for some
help in buttoning the back of her dress:

B: Now the buttons!

S: I can't do nothing with them.

B: You men with your big clumsy fingers. May I have a drag
on your cig?

S: Have one for yourself.

B: Why thanks! . . . It looks like my trunk has exploded.

S: Me an' Stella were helping you unpack.

B: Well, you certainly did a fast and thorough job of it!

S: It looks like you raided some stylish shops in Paris.

B: Ha-ha! Yes—clothes are my passion!

S: What does it cost for a string of fur-pieces like that?

B: Why, those were a tribute from an admirer of mine!

S: He must have had a lot of—admiration!

B: Oh, in my youth I excited some admiration. But look at me now! Would you think it possible that I was once considered to be—attractive?

S: Your looks are okay.

B: I was fishing for a compliment, Stanley.

S: I don't go in for that stuff.

It may well be that, aside from the outlandish wardrobe, words are all Blanche has left in the world. Within a few short remarks, however, she tests Stanley out, commenting on his "big clumsy fingers," asking for a "drag" on his "cig," bragging about her "admirers" and her "passion" for clothes, and finally admitting she is "fishing for a compliment." Her choice of vocabulary would demand a seductive vocal tone, despite the fact that her well-timed sexual pass is quickly fumbled against Stanley's indifference.

Nevertheless, in a careful reconsideration of this passage we deduce that Blanche's Southern aristocratic background is a reality of the past. Perhaps her desperate manner reflects a fall from grace, making her vulnerable to the "kindness of strangers," as she will admit later in the play. We are likely to *hear* her, in this passage, as the stereotypical Southern belle she pretends to be, with a delicately affected *drawl*—a manner of speech characterized by slowness and prolongation of syllables—behind which she can mask her vulnerability. Stanley provides a harsh dramatic contrast in his refusal to cooperate, that is, to play the Southern gentleman. His straightforward manner and ungrammatical speech have been learned in the street. His tone is abrasive and, as a dramatic vocal contrast to Blanche, lacks the compassion she needs to hear. If regionalism exposes Blanche as a tragic, faded beauty who has "gone astray," it strengthens her no-nonsense adversary as a beast on the prowl.

Pace

Our final component incorporates the essential function of *timing*, the connected rhythms that quicken and halt stage characters in their speech, the dramatic pause that unexpectedly turns to silence. Although we seem to be at a slight disadvantage as playreaders, needing the timing of two actors to facilitate this effect, we can reflect on our own patterns of conversational speech, discovering a workable rhythm that lends energy, contrast, and meaning to our chatter and enhancing our appreciation of this essential component.

Let us *hear* ourselves responding to Beckett's "pauses" and "silences," while reading aloud these final lines from the conclusion of *Waiting for Godot*, in which Estragon and Vladimir contemplate their future:

E: What's wrong with you?

V: Nothing.

E: I'm going.

V: So am I.

E: Was I long asleep?

V: I don't know.

[*Silence.*]

E: Where shall we go?

V: Not far.

E: Oh yes, let's go far away from here.

V: We can't.

E: Why not?

V: We have to come back tomorrow.

E: What for?

V: To wait for Godot.

E: Ah! [*Silence.*] He didn't come?

V: No.

E: And now it's too late.

V: Yes, now it's night.

E: And if we dropped him? [*Pause.*] If we dropped him?

V: He'd punish us. [*Silence.*]

Our approach to this exchange should be likened to the mechanics of breathing: the coordination of inhalations and exhalations measured against each vocalized line. Yet the matter is not so simple as that, despite Beckett's deceptively helpful "silences." Notice how an unindicated long pause, called a *dramatic pause,* inserted *before* Vladimir's response to Estragon's opening question, can alter the literal meaning of the exchange that follows. It might suggest, to the contrary, that something *is* wrong, allowing pace to expose an alternate meaning or imply that what the characters are *saying* may not always reflect what they *mean.* An effective handling of pace, characterized by carefully positioned dramatic pauses, evokes the right touch of ambiguity or mystery in the verbal exchange.

The complexity of Beckett's spiritual premise, in which Estragon and Vladimir continually exchange their roles as perpetrator and victim, cannot be separated from their physical predicament. Estragon's short, staccato-like questions—seven in all—are matched by Vladimir's responses. A sensitive pacing comments on this intricate relationship and informs us that plans have gone askew: Godot may never arrive. Estragon's final question, which is echoed *after* an indicated pause, then followed by Vladimir's response, confirms their desperate dilemma.

An altered pace characterizes the following conversation in *The Basic Training of Pavlo Hummel,* in which Rabe asks us to hear—and respond to—the verbal crossfire of two characters whose relationship evolves from this initial encounter. A black army commander named Ardell questions a young recruit named Pavlo:

> A: Now what's your unit? Now shout it out.
>
> P: Second of the Sixteenth, First Division, BIG RED ONE!
>
> A: Company.
>
> P: Bravo.
>
> A: CO?
>
> P: My company commander is Captain M. W. Henderson. My battalion commander is Lieutenant Colonel Roy J. S. Tully.
>
> A: Platoon?
>
> P: Third.
>
> A: Squad.

P: Third.

A: Squad and platoon leaders.

P: My platoon leader is First Lieutenant David R. Barnes; my squad leader is Staff Sergeant Peter T. Collins.

A: You got family?

P: No.

A: You lyin', boy.

P: One mother; one half brother.

A: All right.

P: Yes.

The "columnized" pattern of the prose dialogue, not unlike the versification of poetic dialogue observed earlier, is our first important clue to its sound and meaning. We notice how a routine investigation, harmless under most circumstances, becomes an assault by Ardell, whose black English—an aspect of his regionalism—sets him apart from Pavlo's youthful "whiteness." In this face-to-face verbal duel, known as *stichomythia*, there is no patience for slip-up or hesitation. Staccato questions must be followed by staccato replies, as if both characters shared the same breath or spoke from the same mouth. The effect of this rapid-fire pacing, coordinated with split-second reaction, is to ensnare the young protagonist in the first of several lies, to suggest that he is a victim and, like Estragon and Vladimir, may find no way out.

Themes for Analysis: Hearing Stage Characters

The acoustical components of character dialogue must be assessed according to *articulation, timbre, regionalism,* and *pace.* Of course, the importance of one component over another can be determined only by the individual drama and characters under discussion. As we expand our knowledge of certain recognizable character types and the writing styles of specific playwrights, we will grow more adept at hearing as well as visualizing them. In the meantime, let us test our ability to "sound out" certain stage characters who are noticeably distinguished by these components and, therefore, provide us with ample opportunity for discussion and analysis:

1. The comic character of Lady Bracknell in Wilde's *Importance of Being Earnest* is opinionated, authoritative, and scrupulous. Suggested theme: "What Lady Bracknell's Vocal Mannerisms Reveal in *The Importance of Being Earnest.*"

2. In Euripides's *Trojan Women*, the character of Cassandra is deranged and ravaged by war. Suggested theme: "The Voice of Sorrow, Loss, and Defeat as Expressed in Cassandra's Monologue from *The Trojan Women.*"

3. Influencing the way we "hear" his characters, Pinter indicates nearly one hundred "pauses" and a half-dozen "silences" in act 1 of his play, *The Homecoming*. Suggested theme: "Playing Dramatic Pauses for Meaning in *The Homecoming.*"

4. In Chekhov's *Three Sisters*, the characters of Masha, Irina, and Olga possess distinctively different personalities and convictions. In scenes they share together, however, a special rhythm or balance characterizes their blended voices, uniting them even further. Suggested theme: "The Effects of Vocal Interplay among the Prozorov Sisters in *The Three Sisters.*"

5. In a play-within-a-play framework, Bottom and his five fellow mechanicals act out a very funny "Pyramus and Thisbe" sequence toward the conclusion of Shakespeare's *Midsummer Night's Dream*. Much of the farcical humor emerges from *how* the characters say their lines, as well as how they portray their "rehearsed" characters in the sequence itself. Suggested theme: "Hearing Six Distinct Comic Voices in the 'Pyramus and Thisbe' Sequence of Shakespeare's *Midsummer Night's Dream.*"

6. The character of Jerry in Albee's *Zoo Story* reveals detailed information about himself through the timbre, regionalism, and pace of his narrated anecdote titled, "The Story of Jerry and the Dog." Suggested theme: "The Narrating of Jerry's Story as a Clue to His Character in *The Zoo Story.*"

CHAPTER FOUR
SETTING THE STAGE FOR ACTION

Piece out our imperfections with your thoughts.
—*Henry V*, Prologue

The Dramatis Personae

Although it is not always possible to determine which "imperfections" the playwright will ask us to "piece out" first—the characters or the setting—there are important clues to be found in the cast of characters, the list of *dramatis personae*, or "persons of the drama" that traditionally serves as preface to most published texts. As the significance of the list alters from one playwright to another, we must be careful not to ignore whatever shreds of detail might enhance our perception of the play. In the classical Greek and Roman dramas, translators and editors have restored cast lists to conform with contemporary standards, occasionally delineating the characters according to their royal titles (Creon, King of Corinth) or blood relationships (Andromache, widow of Hector). Shakespeare's editors have been unusually helpful in clarifying these relationships for us. In one popular edition of *Hamlet*, for example, the editor lists Claudius as "King of Denmark," Hamlet as "son to the late, and nephew to the present King," and Gertrude as "Queen of Denmark, and mother to Hamlet." In final position on a list that contains more than two dozen speaking roles is this most revealing item: "Ghost of Hamlet's father." Even if we are unacquainted with *Hamlet*, we might suspect at once that this quartet of aristocratic gentry, including an "unearthly" intruder, is a hotbed of conflict and that the lengthy cast of characters mirrors the unusual size and scope of Hamlet's world.

Several Restoration dramatists also paint a helpful and detailed picture of their plays. In *The Way of the World*, Congreve adjoins revealing information to certain characters' names: "Fainall, in love with Mrs. Marwood; Mirabell, in love with Mrs. Millamant; Lady Wishfort, Enemy to Mirabell, for having falsely pretended love to her; Mrs. Millamant, a fine Lady, Niece to Lady Wishfort, and loves

Mirabell." Congreve seems determined to establish for us the political and sexual intrigues of his characters even before we encounter them. We must not overlook his alerting us to the special partnership between Mirabell and Mrs. Millamant that is central to the action.

Modern playwrights seem less willing to share too much information in their character lists. Shaw dispenses with cast lists altogether, preferring to comment on his characters as they enter their respective scenes. Williams is typical of most contemporary playwrights who simply list the characters "in order of appearance," much like the list that appears in the playgoer's playbill. In *The Glass Menagerie*, however, Williams outdoes himself by providing us with more than a dozen sentences in the stage directions that vividly flesh out the physical and emotional profiles of three of the play's four characters, helping us to understand these characters more fully when we encounter them. The same painstaking description embellishes the two-character cast list of Marsha Norman's *'night, mother* (1982), a play that also focuses on a mother-daughter relationship. Where Williams's descriptions are abstract and elusive, Norman's are candid and gritty, telling us exactly how these characters should behave and perceive themselves. It is a major advantage served to the playreader but denied the playgoer.

Symbolic Nomenclature

Although Shakespeare's Juliet asks, "What's in a name? That which we call a rose / By any other name would smell as sweet," the playreader knows much better. The complexity of certain contemporary cast lists, in reflecting the psychological dimensions of modern realism, provokes our consideration of hidden clues in their designation of specific character names. The technique is not unlike the personified virtues and vices who surrounded the medieval Everyman character and behaved according to their titles. Known as *symbolic nomenclature*, this allows the playwright to affix representative names to his characters. In *The Glass Menagerie*, Laura Wingfield's ethereal fragility is reflected by the "aura" and "wing" components of her name, just as this same "sound-sense" accompanies Miller's Willie "Loman," our contemporary Everyman. The protagonist of Elmer Rice's *Adding Machine* (1923) is Mr. Zero, a name that befits his predicament. George Gibbs and Emily Webb in Wilder's *Our Town* bear names of typical small-town American citizens; however, another married couple George and Martha (no last name given!) ironically suggest the symbolic, archetypal labels of George and Martha Washington, the founding father and mother of America in Albee's *Who's Afraid of Virginia Woolf?*.

The fact that "the name's the same" continues to engage our curiosity, even when it is rooted in a foreign word or plays on certain word twists. Theodore "Hickey" Hickman, the salesman who preaches salvation to his alcoholic soulmates in O'Neill's *Iceman Cometh* (1939), is "God's gift," as the Greek words *theos* (God) and *doron* (gift) jointly signify. Hickey's antagonist is named Larry Slade, the grammatical distortion of the past tense of "slay." The booze-dispensing proprietor of the saloon where the action is set is called, somewhat ironically, Harry Hope. The names O'Neill has given these three individuals aptly characterize their pivotal, triangular relationship. With discretion, therefore, a brief study of the possible symbolic reference of nomenclature can enhance our playreading analysis of the purpose and function of certain stage characters.

Character and Stage Descriptions

In much the same way, we should be alerted to the playwright's character descriptions and stage directions for what they tell us about *dramatic action*. Do these directions, or *stage rubrics*, italicized for the playreader's convenience, carry the same weight as character dialogue, or are they just fragmentary guidelines to be followed lightly? Certain stage directors choose to ignore them, preferring to envision their own character types and designs for the play—an approach that is essential in the classical theatre, for example, where stage rubrics are rare or nonexistent. Since each of us, as a playreader, is likely to respond differently to the same set of rubrics, however, we must acknowledge them to discover the playwright's intentions, then reinterpret them to accommodate our own imaginative needs.

Stage directions can vary widely. Notice how simply Beckett sets the stage in *Waiting for Godot*: "A country road. A tree. Evening." A sharp image is etched with an economy of words. He indicates even less about his five characters, trusting that they will reveal themselves through their dialogue. In contrast, the last four sentences—all stage directions—that close Strindberg's *Dream Play* (1907) create a more complex stage picture: "[The daughter] goes into the castle. Music is heard. The background is lit up by the burning castle and reveals a wall of human faces, questioning, grieving, despairing. As the castle breaks into flames, the bud on the roof opens into a gigantic chrysanthemum flower." Following the disconnected but logical form of a dream, Strindberg's images do more than merely suggest scenic atmosphere; they seem to provide the scenario for a film montage as well. They challenge our playreading imagination in much the same way as they would a stage director's, and they encourage our exploring the important *production ingredients* of any play. Above all, Beckett and Strindberg describe the range of scenic efforts we might expect to encounter.

The Simple Setting

In his long one-act play, *The Zoo Story*, Albee introduces characters, setting, and initial character "blocking" (i.e., stage movements) in a compact, sequential order:

> PETER: A man in his early forties, neither fat nor gaunt, neither handsome nor homely. He wears tweeds, smokes a pipe, carries horn-rimmed glasses. Although he is moving into middle age, his dress and his manner would suggest a man younger.
> JERRY: A man in his late thirties, not poorly dressed, but carelessly. What was once a trim and lightly muscled body has begun to go to fat; and while he is no longer handsome, it is evident that he once was. His fall from physical grace should not suggest debauchery; he has, to come closest to it, a great weariness.
> THE SCENE: It is Central Park; a Sunday afternoon in summer; the present. There are two park benches, one toward either side of the stage; they both face the audience. Behind them foliage, trees, sky. At the beginning, Peter is seated on one of the benches.
> (As the curtain rises, Peter is seated on the bench stage-right. He is reading a book. He stops reading, cleans his glasses, goes back to reading. Jerry enters.)

Albee sets us up for a fairly routine event: the confrontation of two strangers. But his directions are characterized by a certain ambiguity that alerts our assessment of this encounter. Is there some hidden significance to these character descriptions? What conclusions may we draw? Of the two characters, Peter is the less clearly delineated: "neither fat nor gaunt, neither handsome nor homely," he is all or none of the above, even though he appears to be an average type, clearly recognizable, who is slightly differentiated by tweeds, pipe, and horn-rimmed glasses. These suggest a passive demeanor, a sense of well-being that does not strive to be anything else on a quiet Sunday afternoon. The second character, by contrast, is more defined. He is "carelessly" dressed, although Albee does not want us to mistake this for impoverishment. While neither character is established as more important than the other, Jerry is certainly the more attention-getting, the one who has experienced some journey that has brought him to this impasse. A reference to his "fall from physical grace," intriguingly contrasted with "debauchery," further heightens our interest. Describing it as some "great weariness," Albee prompts our desire to know something more about him. As Peter's counterpart, Jerry actively draws us into the play.

The playwright now asks us to visualize the setting. Except for the two park benches, his simple but realistic description never detracts from the action but allows Albee to isolate his characters and ultimately draw us closer to them. As an ironic comment, the serene Sunday setting thwarts our expectation of what will follow, since Jerry's entrance is also an intrusion on Peter's privacy and space. Perhaps the play's title warns us about animals and territoriality, as if the bench is a potential trap that will not only manipulate the *blocking* of its two occupants but ensnare them as well. Thus, Albee's character and scenic descriptions, like pieces in a puzzle, necessarily prompt our curiosity. The playwright has invented two characters whose very oppositeness will transform their casual acquaintance into a fatal attraction.

Altering Stage Realism

In contrast with Albee's uncomplicated realism, Miller describes a technically complex set as a key to character, mood, and theme in *Death of a Salesman:*

The curtain rises. Before us is the Salesman's house. We are aware of towering, angular shapes behind it, surrounding it on all sides. Only the blue light of the sky falls upon the house and forestage; the surrounding area shows an angry glow of orange. As more light appears, we see a solid vault of apartment houses around the small, fragile-seeming home. An air of the dream clings to the place, a dream rising out of reality.

Miller's poetic description of Willie Loman's neighborhood is rich in detail. Selected references to "angular shapes," the "angry glow of orange," and the "solid vault" of apartment houses evoke strong feelings of isolation, loneliness, and entrapment, not unlike those expressed in *The Zoo Story*. We must make no mistake in recognizing this as the home of Miller's protagonist. That a "dream clings to the place" exposes the lack of fulfillment that permeates its inhabitants. Miller describes a simple kitchen, a living room, and two bedrooms, one of which is elevated six and a half feet behind the kitchen. He proceeds to tell us that:

> The entire setting is wholly or, in some places, partially transparent. . . . Whenever the action is in the present the actors observe the imaginary wall-lines, entering the house only through its doors at the left. But in the scenes of the past these boundaries are broken, and characters enter or leave a room by stepping "through" a wall onto the forestage.

This "transparent" effect facilitates the mingling of past and present events, supporting the dreamlike ambience that motivates the characters' behaviors. More important, it contributes to the working of "memory" in the actions of the play. The description is also characterized by elements of *expressionism,* a technique that allows Miller to reflect—through the use of one-dimensional, angular set designs—the fragmented emotional state of his protagonist. Finally, the half-realistic setting comments on the play's central theme: that a false or distorted reality can underlie one's personal success.

Expressionism

An overt example of expressionism may be found in Eugene O'Neill's *Hairy Ape* (1922), where the protagonist, Yank, toils with his mates in a cramped space:

. . . in the bowels of a ship, imprisoned by white steel. The lines of bunks, the uprights supporting them, cross each other like the steel framework of a cage. The ceiling crushes down upon the men's heads. They cannot stand upright.

Unlike Miller, who uses expressionistic and nonrealistic touches to suggest a mood or highlight his characters, O'Neill's heavy reliance on a physically distorted stage set mirrors the brutish behavior and emotional turmoil of Yank, who admits he "ain't on oith and I ain't in heaven, get me? I'm in de middle tryin' to separate 'em, takin' all de woist punches from bot' of 'em. Maybe dat's what dey call hell, huh?" As a theatrical style in which the artist imposes his own personal description of reality on the outside world, expressionism supports O'Neill's theme of the outsider and isolates a protagonist who struggles desperately to "belong."

Realism, Symbolism, and Dramatic Foreshadowing

As a realistic playwright, Ibsen describes a "large handsomely furnished drawing room" to serve each of the four acts of Hedda Gabler (1890). The back wall of the room further opens "to a smaller room decorated in the same style as the drawing room." The rooms are filled with plush sofas, high-back armchairs, hanging lamps, and expensive ornaments. A strong, almost masculine sense of well-being predominates. But Ibsen also knows that a strict adherence to a realistic style would prevent him from underscoring for us some very important nonverbal clues. He realizes that total realism in itself is unattainable and meaningless. Therefore, he includes one particular prop—"the portrait of a handsome elderly man in the uniform of a general"—which hangs above the sofa and provides an ironic touch to the atmosphere. There is *symbolic* value to this portrait of Hedda's father, the late General Gabler. As a major scenic "symbol," it serves to represent the pathological father-daughter relationship that has fashioned Hedda's ruthless and self-destructive nature.

If we are perceptive enough to grasp the symbolic evidence amid the realistic clutter of the Gabler household, our insight into character relationships is enhanced through further symbolic detailing. Ibsen tells us that Hedda is a woman of twenty-nine whose "face and figure show breeding and distinction. Her complexion is pale and opaque.

Her eyes are steel-gray and express a cold, unruffled repose. Her hair is an agreeable medium-brown, but not especially abundant." Nor can we ignore his description of her rival, the younger Thea Elvsted, who is "a fragile woman with soft, pretty features. Her large, round, light-blue eyes are slightly prominent and have a timid, questioning look. Her hair is unusually fair, almost white-gold and extremely thick and wavy." Early in the play, therefore, Ibsen's description of both women foreshadows the play's outcome. These strongly contrasting characters, vying for the love of the same man, are first set off by their steel gray versus light blue eyes. They are finally exposed by one striking physical detail: Hedda's "not especially abundant" hair symbolizes her barren state, while Thea's "thick and wavy" hair symbolizes her fertility and her nurturing relationship with Hedda's former lover, Eilert Lovborg.

Character as Key to Setting

Some of the most challenging clues to onstage events are often indicated by the characters themselves. Working with minimal stage sets in the daylight, and without the benefit of a stage curtain to indicate the necessary scenic changes, Shakespeare had no choice but to explore the versatility of his characters' dialogue so that it not only conveyed meaning to other characters in the play but also alerted his spectators. We share the same responsibility, as playreaders, when we approach Elizabethan drama. When Oberon, the king of the fairies in Shakespeare's *Midsummer Night's Dream* (1595), wishes to remain unseen by some real-world characters who approach nearby, he simply declares: "I am invisible, and I will overhear their conference." The built-in stage direction that renders him invisible is realistically impossible to achieve. However, accepting this stage convention, which makes the impossible quite possible, we willingly cooperate and imagine him unseen by the approaching intruders. Having fled from court with her cousin Celia in *As You Like It* (1599), Rosalind announces "Well, this is the forest of Arden," and lets the playreader know exactly where the present action is set.

When Othello prepares to murder Desdemona, his soliloquy discloses signals vital to the development of the action. In act 5, scene 2, he enters his wife's bed chamber and speaks:

> Yet I'll not shed her blood,
> Nor scar that whiter skin of hers than snow
> And smooth as monumental alabaster.
> Yet she must die, else she'll betray more men.

What clues are contained in these two statements? That Othello is there for the purpose of killing Desdemona without shedding her blood establishes his cautious, premeditated, perhaps encircling approach to her bed; and that Desdemona possesses the whitest and smoothest skin, in contrast with his own dark complexion and even darker purpose. He urges himself to action:

> Put out the light, and then put out the light.
> If I quench thee, thou flaming minister,
> I can again thy former light restore,
> Should I repent me. But once put out thy light,
> Thou cunning'st pattern of excelling nature,
> I know not where is that Promethean heat
> That can thy light relume. When I have plucked the rose,
> I cannot give it vital growth again,
> It needs must wither. I'll smell it on the tree.

Her complexion is illuminated by candle or torchlight, which Othello has carried with him into the chamber. A possible alternative suggests that the light has been positioned at Desdemona's bedside *prior* to his entering the room. What will his next course of action be? First, to put out the candlelight, which he now holds up to her face, to create the appropriate darkness in which to carry out the deed; second, to extinguish *her* light, a symbol of the vital breath in her body. Since he has promised not to shed her blood nor scar her alabaster skin, this will be accomplished either by strangulation, with hands clenched around her neck, or by simply holding a pillow over her face. Othello hesitates, reflecting momentarily on the absolute finality of extinguishing her breath. Then he continues to speak:

> Ah, balmy breath, that doth almost persuade
> Justice to break her sword! One more, one more.
> Be thus when thou art dead, and I will kill thee,
> And love thee after. One more, and this the last.
> So sweet was ne'er so fatal. I must weep,

But they are cruel tears. This sorrow's heavenly,
It strikes where it doth love. She wakes.

Now Desdemona apparently faces upward, allowing us to see or at least to imagine her more clearly. The fact that Othello can actually smell her balmy breath tells us how physically close his face is next to hers. Perhaps he lifts her head off the pillow and cradles it in his arms in an effort to be closer to her. Or perhaps he wishes to kiss her just "one more" time. Indeed, he is suddenly tempted to kiss her lips and does. So overcome is he, however, that a single embrace is not enough. He embraces her once more, so passionately this time that he is moved to tears and accidentally awakens her. In twenty lines of verse Othello has not only delivered a haunting and powerful pretext for murdering his wife but has carefully, set the scene, described his and Desdemona's physical appearances, and ultimately devised a cohesive piece of "stage blocking" for our imagination to feed on.

Musical Sound Effects

The atmosphere of theatrical illusion, like that of real life, is composed of stage pictures, characters, words, and sounds. The last of these is hardly the least, for the detail of any setting is frequently embellished by the occurrence of carefully designated sound effects. Music and noise, of both specific and nondescript varieties, constitute the traditional sound effects that enhance the mood and action of any drama. Before the curtain rises on the towering and angular shapes we observed earlier in *Death of a Salesman*, Miller indicates that "a melody is heard, played upon a flute. It is small and fine, telling of grass and trees and the horizon." The nondescript tune is secondary to the more important requirement that it be played softly on a particular instrument—the flute—to suggest something eternal as it carries us back to a time and place somewhere in our imagination. Having established this personal and evocative mood, the melody lingers as the curtain ascends on a stage set that contrasts sharply with the haunting rural landscape for which the music has prepared us. Thus, the playwright's jarring juxtaposition of musical sounds and stage images escorts us into the similarly conflicted Loman household.

In *A Streetcar Named Desire*, Williams allows a specific melody, in this case the "Varsouviana" polka, to symbolize a definite mood and setting and to unify the actions associated with it. As a symbolist, Williams frequently uses words, characters, and stage images to reflect another time or place. It has been carefully established in the play that the young man to whom Blanche Dubois was once married, but whom we never meet, shot himself in the head while the "Varsouviana" played in the background. For years Blanche has tried to forget the painful circumstances that motivated the tragic event. But she has found no refuge. When her feelings of entrapment increase during the later scenes of the play, Williams indicates that "the 'Varsouviana' faintly plays"; then it "is playing distantly," and finally, it "rises audibly" and is accompanied by "a distant revolver shot." This last occurrence coincides with Blanche's own mental disintegration while the playwright reminds us that "the music is in her mind."

Noisy Sound Effects

The distant gunshot in *Streetcar* becomes, once again, the single and perfectly timed sound effect heard by all of the characters assembled in the drawing room at the conclusion of Ibsen's *Hedda Gabler*. Without attempting to create a mood or reflect some hidden meaning, Ibsen simply informs us that "a shot is heard within." Only seconds earlier, however, he has given his protagonist the chance to set her scene: Hedda momentarily excuses herself and withdraws to an inner room, carefully closing the curtain behind her. An earlier reference in the play to her fascination for the late General Gabler's pistols hardly foreshadows the irrational, self-destructive act about to take place. When we hear the pistol shot, there is great irony in the fact that we, as playreaders or spectators, do not register the same astonishment as the characters in the scene do. But the sound jolts us nevertheless. Disruptive in its suddenness, painfully noisy at such close range, swift in its fatal impact, it is a cold, spiteful, attention-getting response to a life that has become unbearable to live.

But sound effects can also impart symbolic meaning to the action and theme of the play. In Chekhov's *Cherry Orchard* (1904), a devastating piece of news is soon evident to all: Ranevskaya's estate, prized for its magnificent cherry orchard, has been sold to the highest bidder; so her family must vacate, with the expectation of either confronting further disorder or rebuilding their lives elsewhere. As if to comment on the events that have precipitated this dreaded impasse, Chekhov incorporates a stage direction of unusual symbolic dimension:

A distant sound is heard that seems to come from the sky, the sound of a snapped string mournfully dying away. A stillness falls, and nothing is heard but the thud of the ax on a tree far away in the orchard.

It should not matter to us how qualitative or resonant this "snapped string" is. Perhaps the effect is nothing more than a tightly pulled violin string breaking discordantly offstage, then echoing and fading. Not meant to be perceived by the characters, this stroke is intended for us. It is a sign that an irretrievable era of history has ended and that the occasion is indeed a mournful one. The sudden "thud of the ax" confirms the close of this family's journey or the possible beginning of a new one. Chekhov's theme concerns the cycle of decline, death, and regeneration symbolized by the two carefully chosen sound effects he shares with us.

Costume Effects

Our imaginative responses to character descriptions, scenic designs, and sound effects are uniquely embellished by the costume fabrics and color tones that complement the characters of the play. But once again, many playwrights provide us with few details as they introduce their characters. In classical drama, for example, a conventional approach required that the costuming conform with the period in which the play was set. Classical Greek drama incorporated a stark appearance to serve the physical stage conventions: the mask of tragedy or comedy; a loosely draped garment; and elevated stage shoes. In Elizabethan drama—centuries before modern stage directors decided to make Shakespeare our contemporary by altering the time, place, and character fashions suggested by his plays—an adherence to historical accuracy through both specialized and period costuming was mandatory. The timeless flexibility of his characters and themes have tempted modern stage practitioners to refashion these traditional approaches: for example, *Julius Caesar* (1599) performed in navy blue business suits; *Much Ado about Nothing* (1599) costumed in the trappings of the late nineteenth-century American Southwest; *The Merchant of Venice* (1597) tailored in the posh elegance of the twentieth-century Italian Riviera. Conforming to the stage conventions of its own time, however, the contemporary play must demonstrate an unaffected realism through stage characters who dress accordingly.

Dressing for Status

Without allowing excessive fashion details to distract our focus from the drama itself, playwrights often furnish us with important costuming details concerning character, action, and theme. Aside from the obvious need to clothe a character's nakedness, the most important effect of a costume is its designation of rank or status, both political and economic, to the character. Brutus Jones, the chain-gang escapee of O'Neill's *Emperor Jones* (1920), has set himself up as emperor of an island in the West Indies. A tall, powerfully built, middle-aged black man, he wears a "light-blue uniform coat, sprayed with brass buttons, heavy gold chevrons on his shoulders, gold braid on the collar, cuffs, etc. His pants are bright red, with a light-blue stripe down the side." Jones also wears "patent leather laced boots with brass spurs." Within the course of several hours, in the midst of a jungle clearing, Jones's shoes are "cut and misshapen, flapping about his feet," while his pants "have been so torn away that what is left of them is no better than a breech cloth." O'Neill asks us to measure his protagonist's fall from power—a literal journey that symbolically records his struggle to "belong"—by the disintegration of his clothing.

Just as Brutus Jones is stripped of his rank, Eliza Doolittle's first-act status as flower girl "in a shoddy black coat that reaches nearly to her knees" and covers a "brown skirt with a coarse apron" is radiantly elevated to that of a duchess "in opera cloak, brilliant evening dress, and diamonds, with fan, flowers, and all accessories," in Shaw's *Pygmalion* (1913). Although we quickly acknowledge that it has taken more than a mere change of clothing to create this new Eliza, the transformation is so successful that it practically unhinges the character most responsible for it, Professor Henry Higgins, and sustains Shaw's lively battle-of-the-sexes theme.

Dressing for Mood

Costumes may also correspond with the *mood,* or emotional status, that befits the character. When the schoolmaster, Medvedenko, speaks the first line of Chekhov's *Sea Gull* (1896), it is in the form of a question addressed to Masha: "Why do you always wear black?" "I am in mourning for my life. I am unhappy," she replies, telling us a good deal about her physical character and emotional makeup and even more about the spiritual malaise or uneasiness that permeates the play.

Above all, Chekhov's opening lines foreshadow the tragic circumstances that follow and highlights its ironic label, "a comedy in four acts." Although there may be some need to elucidate his definition of comedy, there is no lack of irony in the sustained and mournful facade—mirrored through a simple costume effect—he has invested in this character.

If Chekhov's special brand of realism, enhanced by subtle, mood-inspiring costume effects, represents one extreme, then Adrienne Kennedy's montage of surreal stage figures literally dazzles our imagination in her long one-act play, *Funnyhouse of a Negro* (1962). The hallucinatory, emotional state of the protagonist, Sarah, who is "dressed in a white nightgown," is fragmented into several stage characters "dressed in royal gowns of white, a white similar to the white of the [stage] curtain, the material [made of] cheap satin." Sarah's spiritual "selves" are bathed in a "strong white light, while the rest of the stage is in strong unnatural blackness." The jarring juxtaposition of black and white lighting and costuming effects establishes a nightmarish mood symbolic of Sarah's dilemma: her inability to accept a black identity in a white America.

Dressing for Theatrical Effect

While Kennedy's extensive use of white costumes is strictly mood-enhancing, Wilder's restrained use of the color serves an effect that is primarily theatrical. In the third-act funeral scene of *Our Town*, the dead, somberly dressed, are positioned on one side of the stage, and the mourners, hidden under black umbrellas, are positioned on the other side. Suddenly Emily appears in a white dress and stands among the black umbrellas. Her hair hangs down her back and is tied by a white ribbon. The theatrical effect of her whiteness highlights her appearance against a monochromatically darkened background. The additional youthful white ribbon, however, corresponds with her spiritual return to Grover's Corners on the occasion of her twelfth birthday—a final wish that is granted to her before she settles among the dead.

A more resounding theatrical effect is achieved in Sam Shepard's description of Crow's costume in *The Tooth of Crime* (1972): "He wears high-heeled green rock and roll boots, tight greasy blue jeans, a tight yellow t-shirt, a green velvet coat, a shark tooth earring, a silver swastika hanging from his neck and a black eye-patch covering the left eye." Branded with the identifiable markings of a cartoonish cult figure who inhabits a violent and surreal world, Crow's apparel exudes a narcissism that seems perfectly matched by Hoss, his competitor, who is dressed in "black rocker gear with silver studs and black kid gloves." Such outrageous costuming enhances and agitates their deadly act 2 confrontation.

If costumes serve to alter or disguise the characters who wear them, their *absence* can impart a special meaning as well. In Peter Shaffer's *Equus* (1973), the behavior of the emotionally disturbed young man, Alan, is examined through flashback in his brief relationship with a young woman named Jill. The playwright's description of their sexual encounter seems appropriately discreet and ritualized: "She lifts her sweater over head: he watches—then unzips his. They each remove their shoes, their socks, and their jeans. Then they look at each other diagonally across the [stage], in which the light is gently increasing." Their graceful disrobing, mirrored in each other, is intensified, almost clinically, in the gradually increased stage light, reenacting a harmless exchange that precipitates Alan's subsequent downfall. Alan's nakedness symbolizes his vulnerability to the doctor who will ultimately curb his creative but self-destructive passions. Thus his exchange with Jill provokes our awareness that nudity can serve the play's theme and function as theatrical costuming.

Themes for Analysis: Setting the Stage

Starting with the conventional *cast list* and closing with the details of costume descriptions, the critical eye and acute ear can disclose important *production ingredients* that contribute significantly to any successful playreading experience. In question 1, for example, a careful itemization and description of *stage effects,* including some discussion of how each is handled, accurately reveals Wilder's purpose: that a simple, semi-illusionistic physical environment befits the inevitable cycle of life, love, and death. The following list brings a variety of potential themes into focus. Strengthen your responses with careful and exact reference to each of the plays cited. The topics marked with an asterisk are annotated with suggestions in brackets ([ ]) to aid in your research and discussion:

1. "Stage Effects and Their Message in Wilder's *Our Town.*"

*2. "The Relevance of Expressionist Sets in Relation to the Action of Rice's *Adding Machine.*" [Several photographs of the original production exist in certain play anthologies or theatre production texts. Perhaps your librarian can help you find these important documents to facilitate your appreciation and discussion of expressionism in Rice's play.]

*3. "What Symbolic Nomenclature and Detailed Character Descriptions Tell Us in O'Neill's *Iceman Cometh.*" [A quick glance at any major O'Neill biography—in those chapters dealing with the *Iceman,* of course—will elucidate the fascinating *real versus fictional* counterparts relating to nomenclature and character prototypes in this important work.]

4. "Theatrical Costuming in O'Neill's *Hairy Ape.*"

*5. "Real and Imaginary Sound Effects in O'Neill's *Emperor Jones.*" [A popular LP recording of this long one-act play can be secured at most public libraries. Exactly how this listening experience affects your appreciation of the play should be included in your discussion of this topic.]

6. "The Surreal Environment as It Relates to the Black/White Issues in Kennedy's *Funnyhouse of a Negro.*"

*7. "The Claustrophobic World of Albee's *Zoo Story.*" [The use of a park bench as the focal point of conversation and interaction is not peculiar to Albee's play alone, although Albee has demonstrated its possibilities more impressively than other playwrights have. Therefore, consider the ramifications of the word *claustrophobic* and show how, despite the park setting and the stark positioning of the bench at center stage, both Peter and Jerry are locked into a relationship from which there is no reasonable escape.]

8. "The Effects of Cross-Dressing in Shakespeare's *As You Like It.*"

*9. "Stage Blocking as Dictated through Dialogue in Shakespeare's *Othello.*" [An appropriate way to *demonstrate* your response is to insert your discovery of specific stage blocking—as revealed through character dialogue—in the margins of your personal copy of the text. This will help you see the *frequency* and *extent* of the characters' physical movements in relation to their spoken lines.]

10. "Scenic Descriptions and the Special Moods of Williams's *Glass Menagerie.*"

*11. "Scenic Description and the Use of Flashbacks in Miller's *Death of a Salesman.*" [Show how the elements of expressionism contribute to this work as a "memory play." Consider how Miller could have achieved the same end or purpose through a purer stage realism.]

12. "Realistic Designs versus Symbolic References in Ibsen's *Hedda Gabler.*"

CHAPTER FIVE
DRAMATIC STRUCTURES

I'll lay
A plot shall show us all a merry day.
—*Richard II*, IV, i

What Is Plot?

After introducing the characters and setting to the reader, the playwright arranges the dramatic action into a cohesive design or *plot*. His sharply etched characters, strengthened by dialogue, establish a story line or "message" that will either grip us or, as Shakespeare intends, "show us all a merry day." Our concern for plot incorporates *form* (how the story will unfold) as well as *content* (what the story is about). In the opening action of Shakespeare's *Macbeth* (1606), the Scottish nobleman, Macbeth, encounters three weird sisters who tell him he will soon be king. The incident provides enough *exposition* or informational background to all subsequent events of the play. But in a later confrontation the same nobleman-turned-king meets his bloody death at the hands of camouflaged soldiers who overtake his castle. This before-and-after effect, depicted in two separate actions, demonstrates how plot is determined by the unique interplay of form and content.

Other implications also seem clear: plots are revealed in *time*—not *real* time, which would require many hours to unfold, but *psychological* time, in which a selection of separate stage actions are telescoped to a desirable length. The opening confrontation marked the beginning of Macbeth's ascent to the throne, and the last one dramatized that journey's outcome, reminiscent of the rising and falling actions Aristotle documented in the Greek tragedies. Adhering to this formal recommendation for a single time, place, and action, the plot structure of the typical Greek drama seems fairly unsophisticated to us now, rather like an extended one-act play highlighted by the subtle rhythms of character and choral exchanges. It was, in fact, the *trilogy*, or three-play format, that gave the Greek playwright some flexibility to follow his protagonist from one setting and action to another. Thus, the time, place, and action of Sophocles's *Oedipus at Colonnus* (404 B.C.) all differ from *Oedipus Rex* (426 B.C.), the first play of his Theban trilogy. We must investigate all three plays, including *Antigone* (441 B.C.), if we wish to know more about Oedipus and his cursed family.

The somewhat conservative plot conventions of classical drama inevitably paved the way for more complex structures. Eventually, the playwright allowed himself consecutive units of stage time, or "scenes," to mirror the multiple places, actions, and, of course, time spans his protagonist needed to work out his obstacles, *all within the same play*. Shakespeare's plots were patterned along such lines, each scene delineated and identified by shifts in time, place, and action. The traditional five-act division by which we now recognize these plays was a labeling imposed by scholarly editors who categorized, unified, and clarified these scenic arrangements to aid the reader. As a result, the modern playwright can take much for granted in utilizing whatever dramatic structure will serve his individual purpose. Contemporary playwrights have been known to structure their full-length plays around the two-act format, an awkward concession to commercial taste that accommodates playgoers who do not wish to be inconvenienced by more than one intermission. Nevertheless, the variety of options finally attests to the stamina and durability of plot structures.

The Aristotelian (Dramatic) Model

What unifies this assortment of plot structures, whether classical, Shakespearean, or contemporary, is the Western device of internal (psychological) or external (physical) *conflict*, providing us with both character interaction and story-line complication. This artificial patterning of conflict adds up to *plot*, which Aristotle regarded as the first principle of the drama and the very soul of tragedy. Characters held second place for him. He also insisted on a "tragic flaw" in the protagonist, that is, some weakness that led to his calamities and made him sympathetic to us. As for the plot itself, it should contain three distinct movements:

1. *Complication* or series of rising actions that build toward a climax and create suspense in the spectator.

2. *Recognition* or climax which marks a turning point in the protagonist's journey, as well as an unexpected reversal of his fortune.

3. *Unravelling* or denouement which follows the protagonist's descent from the turning point to his demise.

In the presence of a carefully designed plot, Aristotle believed that the spectator needed only to hear the story of King Oedipus, without seeing it, in order to have the essential ingredients of pity and terror aroused in him. After a series of rising actions surrounding his birth and status, Oedipus confronts a messenger who, he believes, will free him from his worst fears: that he has unknowingly murdered his father and married his mother. But this moment of recognition, which the playreader identifies as the *climax*, is coincidental with the *reversal*, demonstrating that what Oedipus feared most has already happened: an irony that precipitates his tragic downfall.

What Is the Deus ex Machina?

Although Aristotle admired Sophocles's effective interplay of actions, he scorned other dramatic examples in which the series of plotted actions did not progress logically toward some natural outcome. The convention, known as *deus ex machina* (literally translated as "god from the machine"), occasionally rescued the protagonist from his unresolved predicament in a denouement that was artificial and not credibly motivated through the rising actions of the play. Thus, Aristotle faults Euripides's *Medea,* in which the vengeful heroine is mercifully rescued by the sympathetic deity. On the other hand, the workings of fate, as long as they are developed through character, are acceptable to any play's outcome. A reader of Sophocles's work, for example, knows how impossible it is to discuss the character of Oedipus without some consideration of the role fate plays.

In the modern theatre, the protagonist who is happily rescued at the last moment by some unforeseen character or situation is pretty much regarded as a weakness of plot structure. However, an effective modern example occurs in the final act of *The Cherry Orchard:* on the exact day his debts are due, the penniless Pishchik announces that an Englishman has paid him a considerable sum for the white clay on his property and wishes to mine the substance for Pishchik's financial gain as well. The

Pishchik incident also represents another stage device, known as *comic relief*, that allows Chekhov to offset the tragic loss of Ranevskaya's estate and the destruction of the prized cherry orchard. The brief intrusion of humor in the midst of weightier dramatic circumstances has remained a long-standing and popular convention of certain plots.

Discovering the Theme

The plot, or the arrangement of the play's actions, cannot be separated from its *theme*, the representation of the central point or underlying message of the play. Often there are several *motifs*, or smaller themes, that contribute to the central one. The ancient Greeks grew up on the legend of Oedipus but never tired of hearing about the murder, incest, suicide, and self-mutilation—a cluster of powerful motifs—that became woven into its plot. That one of their playwrights should choose to dramatize the events of this popular legend finally allowed the ancient Greeks to experience its central *thematic* implication: *that a person's fate is unalterable.*

Our discovery of the psychological and moral implications of a play's theme requires thoughtful consideration of its characters and actions. Certain general themes pervade a wide sampling of dramatic literature: good versus evil; survival of the fittest; the battle of the sexes; the power of love; the quest for selfhood; among others. Although we may begin to surmise the play's underlying purpose, it helps to focus on a central theme that is uniquely characteristic of the work itself. Some helpful clues that point to theme are occasionally stated by the characters themselves. A shepherd warns Oedipus to "make no mistake: you are a doom-born man." In the contemporary play *A Streetcar Named Desire*, Blanche senses defeat at the hands of her brother-in-law, Stanley Kowalski, and warns her sister: "Don't—don't hang back with the brutes!" Her rejection of the forces of darkness, so central to the play, eloquently expresses its theme.

Aristotle and the Elizabethans

Although Shakespeare implemented certain aspects of the Aristotelian design, such as an adherence to the pattern of "rising and falling actions," he significantly advanced his plot structures, as demonstrated in the tragedy of *Othello*. This noble soldier, admired for his great but simple virtues, has recently married Desdemona. His fatal flaw, that he believes all men are what they seem, underlies his downfall. Through the machinations of his jealous confidant, Iago, Othello is "set up" to believe that his wife is sleeping with Michael Cassio. The turning point is a conversation Othello overhears in which Cassio speaks openly about his own mistress, Bianca, whom Othello interprets to mean Desdemona. Generated by his madness and desire for revenge, Othello's "unraveling" leads to an external conflict, resulting in his murder of Desdemona. Only during the final moments of the play's five-act structure, however, does the protagonist recognize his error, at which point he fatally stabs himself. But the outcome also focuses on Iago, the villainous survivor now taken captive, whose personification of evil, matched against the goodness of Othello and the innocence of Desdemona, underscores the central theme of this play: *the power of human corruption through jealousy in love.*

Plot versus Dramatic Irony

Incorporated within *Othello*'s plot structure is the playwright's effective use of *dramatic irony,* which allows us to know more about certain characters and stage actions than the characters themselves do. Although the effects of dramatic irony vary from play to play, they function consistently here in exposing Iago's internal conflict: his need to arouse jealousy in Othello. In the first scene, for example, Iago confides in Roderigo, "I am not what I am," while disclosing his intentions to work injustices against the Moor. The use of dramatic irony reaches its highest point when, in the midst of steadily rising complications—all engineered by Iago—Othello says of him, "This fellow's of exceeding honesty, / And knows all qualities, with a learned spirit, / Of human dealings." That Othello truly believes all men are what they seem is attributed to his flaw. But such gullibility is all the more tragic when it is so cruelly manipulated.

Analogous Actions

As an innovator of style, Shakespeare transcended strict adherence to Aristotelian form and further devised a multiplicity of plot structures or *analogous actions.* We witness its definitive use in *King Lear,* a play that is notable for the unusual order of its rising and falling actions. The story concerns an aged monarch who decides to divide his kingdom among three daughters in proportion to the degree of love each can express for him. Barely fifty lines into the first act, Lear asks: "Which of you shall we say doth love us most?" While Goneril and Regan exaggerate their expressions of love, the youngest, named Cordelia, answers with one word: "Nothing"—but assures him she loves him "according to [her] bond, nor more nor less." Lear's reaction, that "nothing will come of nothing," voices his complete misunderstanding of Cordelia's response and devotion, a catalytic plot complication that sets the tone of the tragedy early on.

Lear's complex relationship with his daughters is sharply mirrored by another in the play: old Gloucester's relationship with a legitimate son named Edgar and with an illegitimate one called Edmund. Shakespeare's careful paralleling of plot structures is much more than a balancing of character types (two aged fathers settling scores with good and evil children) and theme (the endurance of human love). He has constructed a major plot (Lear) that is tightly interwoven with a minor one (Gloucester) and through their *analogous actions and interactions* allows each to comment on the other. Only in his madness does Lear reason out the true natures of Goneril and Regan, shortly before Gloucester, in his blindness, recognizes Edmund's treachery. This turning point, occurring in the play's crucial third act, also marks Lear's awareness of Cordelia's loyalty and love. Although this recognition cannot rescue her from an unhappy fate, revealed in the final moments of the play, it allows Lear to be reconciled with her through peaceful death.

Plot versus Subplot

While the minor Gloucester plot is analogous to the major Lear one, beginning later and ending earlier than Lear's story, it functions in a subordinate position and becomes a *subplot* within the total structure. Of course, this network of plots and subplots is not unusual in Elizabethan drama, especially in the plays of Shakespeare. A striking variation occurs in *A Midsummer Night's Dream*, where numerous subplots are carefully interwoven, yet each functions independently and none is directly analogous to the other. The problems Bottom and his friends encounter in the rehearsal of their dramatic playlet to be presented at the marriage of Theseus and Hippolyta, for example, neither reflect nor directly affect the subplot that depicts Titania's relationship with Oberon or the one that unravels the tangled romantic affairs of Lysander, Demetrius, Hermia, and Helena. We are always aware of the playwright's skill at keeping each of these subplots in focus, merging their respective outcomes only at the play's conclusion. Although *A Midsummer Night's Dream* deals with the complexities of subplot and character relationships, its final integrated view is essential to its "wholeness-through-love" theme.

Plotting the Well-Made Play

Although Aristotle had very little to say about comic plots, it is not surprising that his theory should influence their development as well. One of those indirectly influenced was Bernard Shaw, a playwright who was hardly an imitator; he brought realism to the English stage and revitalized the drama when new themes and techniques were sorely needed. But in his three-act comedy *Arms and the Man* (1894), he could not resist fashioning a set of predictible characters into a *well-made* plot structure that is perfectly executed in its arrangement of complication, recognition, and denouement. The scene is Bulgaria in 1885 and 1886. After a battle in which her country has been victorious, a young woman, Raina, harbors an enemy soldier in her bedroom. She neither asks for his name, nor does he volunteer it. But there is an instant attraction between them, in spite of the fact that her father, Major Petkoff, and her fiancé, Sergius, most likely fought against him. By the close of their first act encounter, Shaw's premise bubbles with humorous implications.

In the second act, peace has been declared. The mysterious young soldier, Bluntschli, comes to the Petkoff home to return the coat he received from Raina to help disguise him in his escape. The major and Sergius not only recognize Bluntschli as a professional soldier who fights only when he cannot avoid it, but they greet him most affectionately. Shaw's supreme use of *comic irony* emerges in this act, as the camaraderie of the three "braggart soliders" is reestablished prior to Raina's appearance. Thus, her climactic entrance and the discovery that her father and fiancé have befriended the nameless midnight intruder turn first-act implications into third-act complications, as she struggles valiantly to recover from her embarrassment and romantic delusions. Shaw's theme—that the ideals of love and war often prove false—has been demonstrated in a tightly structured comic plot, replete with irony.

Comedy versus Farce versus Black Comedy

Whereas comedy is developed along traditional lines of plot and character, *farce* excites laughter through the mechanical antics of sight gags, coarse wit, and exaggerated incongruities. Although the physical humor that characterizes both Aristophanic and Roman comedy is occasionally merged with farcical ingredients, this physical humor was always sharply contrasted with the intellectual humor that characterized the comedy of the English Restoration, or "comedy of manners." But laughter could also be a serious business, as Aristophanes demonstrated in *Lysistrata* (411 B.C.) (e.g., the constraint on sex as a preventive to war) or as portrayed by Moliere in *Tartuffe* (1669) (e.g., the fashionable ways of religious hypocrisy).

In the modern theatre, playwrights like Joe Orton and Christopher Durang have used the elements of comedy and farce for more subversive ends than their predecessors did. Their plays, which constitute a style known as black comedy, test the boundaries of propriety and admittedly achieve a certain shock value. Orton, an Englishman, is a realist. The comic plotting of his play *Loot* (1966) centers on stolen money, a household coffin, and a displaced cadaver. Plot complications expose a legal system that is no less corrupt than the body snatchers. Durang, an American, is an absurdist. During the sermonized actions of his play *Sister Mary Ignatius Explains It All for You* (1979), the benign Mother Superior is transformed into a tyrannical monster. Among her many acts of moral instruction, she cold-bloodedly shoots a former student, now a professed homosexual, being assured that his recently confessed soul will go "straight" to heaven. Despite two distinctively different styles, the targets emerge from the despair, isolation, and violence of a contemporary society in which no institution remains sacred. Above all, the machinations of their comic plots need not be credibly motivated nor, for that matter, adhere to the well-made structure.

The Brechtian (Epic) Model

Although much of Western drama is essentially Aristotelian in design, modern playwrights and directors have intentionally challenged this view. The most influential opponent was Bertolt Brecht (1898–1956), the playwright-director whose controversial "epic" theory, which integrates both dramaturgical and philosophical (Marxist) concepts, radically altered the form and content of contemporary drama.

The following synopsis helps us appreciate these principal concepts in relation to the traditional "dramatic" model:

Aristotelian [Dramatic]	Brechtian [Epic]
1. Drama appeals to emotions	1. Drama appeals to intellect.
2. Protagonist's relationship is to himself or God.	2. Protagonist's relationship is to society.
3. Spectator gets close to action.	3. Spectator is alienated from action.
4. Katharsis is sought.	4. Katharsis is avoided.
5. Feelings and experiences are on view.	5. Information and arguments are on view.
6. Man's nature is unalterable.	6. Man's nature is alterable.
7. Suspense is sought: interest in what *will* happen.	7. Suspense *is* not sought: interest in what *is* happening.
8. Scene builds upon scene.	8. Episode follows episode.

Brecht's plays, which include *Mother Courage* (1941), *Galileo* (1943), *The Caucasian Chalk Circle* (1948), and, in earlier collaboration with musical composer Kurt Weill, *The Three Penny Opera* (1928) and *The Rise and Fall of the City of Mahagonny* (1930), are intended to demonstrate the principles of "epic" theatre, although his best work often succeeds when he himself does not fully obey his own rules. In recent years, "post-Marxist" strategies have called for a reevaluation of Brecht's contributions, a healthy distancing that has allowed theatre practitioners and critics alike to assess epic theory within its proper historical framework. Nevertheless, Brecht's concepts remain important for helping us, as playreaders, to view the social implications of drama from a non-Aristotelian perspective.

Brecht's Model in Action

In one of his more popular plays, *The Good Woman of Setzuan* (1943), Brecht employs a range of ten *episodes* to tell the story of the prostitute Shen Te, the protagonist and title character, whose kindness to the gods wins her their favor but seriously alters her relationship to society. With a financial reward they bestow on her, Shen Te opens a small tobacco shop, where before too long she is victimized by unscrupulous neighbors and customers. In order to survive she is forced to invent a male cousin, Shui Ta (Shen Te in disguise), whose reasonable but uncharitable nature commands the respect of these parasites and enables the shop to thrive. Although Brecht does not offer a solution, as Shen Te is unable to reconcile these male and female sides of her nature, the predicament points to a disturbing theme or Brechtian "thesis": *it is an immoral world that allows ethical ideals to perish and uncharitable ones to succeed.* But the more disturbing implication is that Shen Te has learned what she must do in order to survive in a wicked world.

It is difficult for us to ignore the sharply etched characters, emotional situations, and imaginative stage conventions that Brecht summons up (as seen in the sudden disappearance of Shen Te, or appearance of Shui Ta). Shen Te's dilemma finally touches us, despite Brecht's intention that our own perceptions *not* be blurred by our emotions. In actual stage production, Brecht's techniques facilitate the necessity of audience alienation from the action: actors are often directed to introduce their real names to us before the play starts to reinforce the idea that they will *represent* rather than *become* the characters; actors direct their dialogue *at* us in order to engage our attention or provoke our internal responses; white lighting is often used to destroy stage illusion, reminding us that we are not in Shen Te's tobacco shop, after all, but in the theatre. These theatrical effects, as demonstrated in performance, can favorably predispose us to the playreading experience that lies ahead, whether it be a Brecht play or a reputable drama influenced by his theory.

Approaching the Brechtian Model

1. *Peruse the script.* Before reading the play, get an impression of its arrangement and length of "scenes." *Good Woman* contains a prologue and several episodes that appear fragmentary. Its episodic nature can provide insight into dramatic format and pace.

2. *Sort out the characters.* The first character we meet is Wong, a narrator who serves an important function. Other character groups include the one-dimensional gods, who are "mouthpieces" for one argument in the play, and the familiar parasites, who represent another. Finally, there is Shen Te, who will reappear as Shui Ta. Brecht asks us to accept Shen Te's two-sidedness as a moral necessity, a survival maneuver that allows her to confront a seemingly unworkable dilemma.

3. *Equate language with the play's structure.* Brecht's prose style is interspersed with bad rhymes, puns, and bumpy verse. Songs interrupt the conversational dialogue, serving as independent commentary on the text, all deliberately designed to distract the reader into *hearing* the "message," or thesis, at all costs.

4. *Explore the ambiguities of the script.* In this play, as in his others, Brecht purposely leaves the action unresolved. His attempt to dramatize a thesis *without climax and resolution* is directly related to the non-Aristotelian structure he offers us. The lack of denouement, replaced here with an open-ended question, should engage our intellectual understanding even if we ultimately choose to reject it. In short, we must not close questions the playwright deliberately leaves open.

Discovering Brecht's Influence

The dramaturgical and philosophical implications derived from Brecht's theory, as well as a consistent application of our newly established guidelines, can embellish our understanding and appreciation of many contemporary plays. Partly because the social, political, and theatrical climates seemed right, a generation of English playwrights emerged during the 1950s to demonstrate a range of dramatic styles and themes that were consciously Brechtian; that is, they showed the influence of Brecht's concepts, if not a strict loyalty to them. In form these plays were characterized by a Brechtian economy of style: for example, minimal set and lighting designs and a de-emphasis of stage props. In Bolt's *Man for All Seasons,* for example, a variety of historical places, none of which is established in scenic detail, provides background to the episodic plot structure. Stage props are minimized. A character called "The Common Man," who fulfills the Brechtian function of narrator, carries as much importance as the protagonist, Sir Thomas More. Except for the fact that our emotional responses are finally drawn to More, the structure of the play owes much to Brecht. In Tom Stoppard's *Rosencrantz and Guildenstern Are Dead* (1966), the two eponymous antiheroes usurp Hamlet's focal position in a humorously Brechtian fashion. Stoppard's dramatic reconsideration of Shakespeare's tragedy emphasizes these two commonplace characters as protagonists in order to assert their social and political functions and alter our earlier "dramatic," Aristotelian-oriented preconceptions of them.

Once our view of modern characters has moved away from the "inner life" realism popularized by Chekhov to a Brechtian materialism, we can anticipate contemporary characters who avoid introspection and externalize their purposes to alter their situations. The themes that engage contemporary playwrights typically mirror the sociopolitical problems of a working-class English society: middle-class protagonists and antiheroes who rebuke the injustices of their social systems and thwart our sympathetic responses in such plays as Osborne's *Look Back in Anger*, Edward Bond's *Saved* (1965), Simon Gray's *Butley* (1971), Peter Shaffer's *Equus*, Hare's *Plenty* (1978), and Caryl Churchill's *Top Girls* (1982). In Europe the Brechtian influence has been prominently displayed in the plays of Friedrich Dürrenmatt (*The Visit*, 1956), Max Frisch (*The Firebugs*, 1958), and Peter Weiss (*Marat/Sade*, 1965), all of which express deeply felt social commitments.

The Brechtian Model versus the Non-Brecht Play

Of these representative titles, none is more striking than Shaffer's *Equus*, particularly in view of the Brechtian model. Shaffer has openly acknowledged the contributions of the play's original director, John Dexter, in reshaping the literary text of the play and influencing our visualization of it. Shaffer's script, mirroring the production ingredients that Dexter introduced, is characterized by an extraordinary economy of style that was influenced mostly by Brecht and by the Japanese Noh. The struggle, or thesis, of *Equus* concerns a psychiatrist's attempt to control, and perhaps destroy, the destructive passions of a psychologically deranged young man who, prior to the start of the action, has entered a stable and, for no apparent reason, blinded the horses sheltered there. To determine what constitutes "normality" is at the center of the playwright's thesis.

Our perusal of the script, influenced by the Brechtian framework, heightens our perceptions of Shaffer's intentions:

1. The action unfolds in thirty-five episodes.

2. The nonrealistic set "resembles a railed boxing ring" surrounded by small benches, while upstage, "forming a backdrop to the whole, are tiers of seats in the fashion of a dissecting theatre."

3. The characters in the play sit on stage throughout the course of the action, joined by members of the audience who sit in the

stage tiers, not unlike members of a jury; spectators and actors are forced to confront each other, diminishing the effect of stage illusion.

4. The psychiatrist-protagonist addresses the audience directly, in the fashion of Narrator; the cast of characters functions as a Chorus.

5. The events of the play are reenacted, rather than relived, allowing an intrusive onstage audience to struggle with the play's open-ended thesis.

In a final stage picture that is decisively Brechtian and recalls the lingering impression of Shen Te, the psychiatrist holds the convulsive body of the young man in his arms, as if to implore our compassion. But Shaffer deliberately leaves the action unresolved. Within its emotional, as opposed to intellectual, framework, however, *Equus* demonstrates a "dramatic" rather than "epic" structure: every attempt has been made to arouse our empathy, and suspense toward some outcome has been openly sought. Nevertheless, Shaffer has molded a series of striking Brechtian concepts into a fulfilling, theatrical whole. In doing so, he represents a solid core of contemporary playwrights whose achievements owe a considerable debt to Brecht.

Mainstream versus Alternative: The *Eclectic* Model

Apart from the new sexual politics that emerged in the 1950s, the social upheaval in the United States during the 1960s and early 1970s instigated a form of theatre that has been called, quite appropriately, "alternative." As opposed to a theatre whose values are traditional, commercial, or "mainstream," alternative theatre incorporates a variety of styles too inconsistent and diverse to categorize. The common denominator for all of them, however, is a certain *eclecticism*—the process that allows its practitioners to pick and choose their performance techniques from whatever dramaturgical and philosophical sources are available. Although the *manifestos*, or rules, for alternative theatre are antimainstream, they have spawned many exciting companies, which have managed to flourish alongside of more conventional forms.

For the playreader who has become accustomed to conventional dramatic structures utilizing fully developed literary scripts—indeed the very stronghold of all Western drama—some radical readjustment is necessary. The alternative model incorporates a theatrical language that is not primarily rooted in logical dialogue but deliberately seeks to be verbally inarticulate. Furthermore, it is *actor-centered* rather than character-centered, placing a greater emphasis on such nonverbal codes as movement and silence. Alternative theatre is often *collective theatre*, finding its shape and message in the improvisatory, or spontaneous, collaborative contributions of its actors and director. The playwright is often subordinate in his role as "recorder" of the group's rehearsal transactions, which slowly evolve into the "performance piece." On the other hand, a chosen playwright may initially present the premise, outline, or *scenario* for a script to his actors and director, anticipating that their experimental contributions will reshape its form and content.

Artaud and the Theatre of Cruelty

Although it is difficult to single out the major influences on alternative theatre, there can be no question that Brecht and Antonin Artaud (1896–1948) are its key spokesmen. If Brecht taught modern theatre about epic realism and demanded a rigid economy in form and content, Artaud sought to revive the ceremonial quality of drama as ritual, to give theatrical performance the dignity that accompanied a religious service, and to abolish its reputation as mere entertainment. Artaud attacked the priorities of spoken dialogue, characteristic of theatre as literature, and sought instead to physicalize emotions and ideas through the movements of the actors. He questioned the relationship between playwright and actor, insisting that the existence of the latter should in no way depend on the former. The theatre should be open to risks, the so-called classics should be rebuked, and violence—through the actor's physicalized emotions—should overcome the spectator. The effect of this emotional upheaval would be "cruel," Artaud maintained, which is why his influential manifestos were collectively referred to as the theatre of cruelty.

Experiencing the Eclectic Model

Although there are numerous influential examples of the eclectic model, in terms of theatre pieces and "collectives"—for example, The

Living Theatre under the direction of Judith Malina and Julian Beck or The Performance Group under Richard Schechner's direction—our consideration of the Open Theatre succinctly incorporates its more accessible characteristics. Under the direction of its founder, Joseph Chaiken, and with "words and structure" by playwright Jean-Claude van Itallie, the Open Theatre's production of *The Serpent* (1968) has established itself as a formidable model of the alternative theatre process. The play is subtitled *A Ceremony*, suggesting to us its ritual nature and unquestionable debt to Artaud. The premise, which was developed over a very lengthy workshop-rehearsal period involving some eighteen performers, reflects their discussions and improvisations on the Book of Genesis, until a carefully recorded verbal text with indicated places for improvisation evolved. Such characters as Adam, Eve, Cain, Abel, a Chorus of women, God, and the Serpent are "represented" rather than "acted" by the performers. In a familiar Brechtian style, elements of the myth are reproduced and pointed to, rather than dramatized, by performers who wear street and rehearsal clothing, work with the economy of a relatively propless empty space, and make no attempt at illusion. Finally, the social consciousness of *The Serpent*, demanding that the story of Genesis should provoke images of upheaval in our own time, incorporates stylized reenactments of the assassinations of John F. Kennedy and Martin Luther King, Jr.

The theme of boundaries—the testing of man's limits—is established in the episode titled "Eve and the Serpent":

> Serpent 1: Is it true?
>
> Serpent 2: It is true?
>
> Serpent 3: That you and he,
>
> Serpent 4: You and he
>
> Serpent 4 and 5: May do anything?
>
> Serpent 2: Anything in the garden you want to do?
>
> Serpent 1: Is that true?
>
> Eve: We may do anything
> Except one thing.
>
> First Woman of the Chorus: We may do anything
> Except one thing.

The repetition, which gradually leads to an overlapping of lines among the different speakers, provides a rhythmic effect further captured in the linear arrangements of the dialogue. The incantation, characterized by the intrusive hissing sounds of the performers, must never appear realistic. In a later sequence, when Eve has "eaten of that which was forbidden," Adam takes his first bite, followed by a second:

> All the actors, in a kind of ecstasy, form the serpent, moving in the same manner as we saw the serpent move with fewer actors earlier. The serpent, as played by all the actors, is still a display of the tree of life. It is seductive and inviting. Then the serpent separates.
>
> A bag of apples is found on one side of the stage. An actor empties it out on the stage. The actors play with the apples, eat them, and carry them out to the audience to share their pleasure with them.

Responding to the "Environmental" Process

As playreaders, we gradually begin to grasp the implication and effect of this enacted ceremony. As the biblical images are directly focused on the relationship between us and the performers, the sense of ritual and community—so vital in both classical Western and Asian dramas—is heightened: by accepting the apples, we partake in the breaking of boundaries and the establishment of newer ones. The occasion calls for a special interaction between performers and playreader, a sharing that is attributed to an *environmental theatre process*, which allows the performers and spectators to occupy the same space. The environmental process often characterizes alternative theatre structures and, in the case of *The Serpent*, strengthens its thematic implications: that we are all participants in the Fall and, having bitten the apple, acknowledge the difference between good and evil.

Our playreading perception of each episode is strengthened when we imagine an informal, almost rehearsal-like structure that is flexible to change whenever we choose to hear or envision one of these episodes. The fact that the performers always represent *themselves*, even when they point us to the characters they "portray," contributes to a less rigid and more spontaneous outcome. It becomes increasingly difficult to remain outside the piece, like the spectator of mainstream theatre who perceives the fixed performance through an imaginary fourth wall. Although it is not the purpose of all alternative theatre to incorporate us in this way, the work of the Open Theatre has effectively provided us with a legacy that continues to influence the experimental/alternative process everywhere. Finally, in retrieving the elements of ritual and community, it heightens our playreading awareness of the effects and dimensions of the drama.

Background to a Feminist Aesthetic

Our historical perspective has revealed a conspicuous absence of women in Western performance until their emergence in Restoration drama. Even the female characters who dominated classical Greek drama were performed by men, further distanced and stylized by masks, while the unmasked, three-dimensional heroines of the later Elizabethan drama were portrayed by men and young boys. The biased patriarchal views of Western society have discounted the contributions of women or relegated them to subordinate positions; in the world of drama their achievements as performers have held priority over their accomplishments as playwrights and directors. If a twenty-five-hundred-year-old tradition of Western drama could produce an Everyman character, then where is his female counterpart?

Art versus Gender

The central issue to surface in the midst of this controversy is posed: "Is art genderless?" That a valid response can point to the existence of a "feminist aesthetic" at once undermines the Aristotelian model that has dominated the Western tradition of drama and encourages us to explore the alternatives. As this model was constructed by a male critic and was based on principles from the works of selected male playwrights, how may we presume that the model even remotely reflects a female aesthetic or sensibility? In addition to those undisputed "masters" of the drama, we must recognize the existence of two subgroups: those few successful women playwrights who have remained oblivious to a feminist aesthetic or have simply refused to acknowledge one; and those playwrights, including certain men, whose feminist concerns have mirrored the sexuality, passions, symbols, and language of women.

Therefore, to analyze any work from a feminist perspective is to call for a reevaluation of established or traditional viewpoints. Our discoveries should then be viewed against the existing depictions of women characters in dramatic literature, with emphasis on such issues as gender bias and stereotyping, which have allowed these characters to emerge distortedly. The feminist argument has generated strong repercussions difficult to ignore. That male playwrights have created a range of powerful women, for example, cannot remedy the fact that so many of them are depicted as helpless creatures or down-and-out victims. Ironically, some of the earliest compelling characters, created by the Greek playwrights, were not portrayed as women motivated by love but as acting out their concerns for family, country, and personal honor.

How can this argument *not* affect our reconsideration of prototypes like Medea and Clytemnestra, and modern characters such as Hedda Gabler or Blanche DuBois, all of whom were created by male playwrights generally acclaimed for their feminist sensibilities? Not surprisingly, even Shakespeare's "rounder" women have not always passed muster. A brief look at Ibsen, a "social dramatist" who, prior to the emergence of feminist considerations, was respected for his compassionate depictions of male and female characters, proves most revealing. A feminist reading of *A Doll's House* would probably disregard its often-cited domestic implications, melodramatic character turns, or theme of Nora Helmer's "selfhood" and focus instead on her victimization and marital bondage. A feminist interpretation finds little consolation in the fact that Nora walks out the door but seriously questions what will happen to her now that the door is forever shut behind her—a consideration Ibsen chose to ignore. A feminist view of Hedda Gabler would hold that Hedda's sexual identity has been grossly distorted by a dominant father and her "mannish" persona is symbolically emasculated in a final self-destructive action.

Aristotle's Antifeminist Aesthetic

Finally, there is the Aristotelian model itself, rooted in conflict, and built on rising actions, climax, and denouement, all characteristic of male physicality and therefore alien to many of those who support a feminist aesthetic. If a woman's psychological makeup allows her to focus on an *interior* life, in addition to her exterior one, it is possible that her arrangement of time and events will reshape the subject matter. In the art of the novel, for example, Virginia Woolf achieved an innovative contemporary style that suited her psychological temperament and inspired a feminist aesthetic long after her work had been accomplished. By the same token, the success of Lillian Hellman, the single conspicuous contemporary American woman playwright who also spent the better part of her career at writing plays, seems oddly disconnected from a feminist ideal. The political concerns that were frequently evident in her plays were rarely sexual, even though they allowed her to compete with the expectations of a patriarchal structure.

Hellman and the Prefeminist Drama

Hellman's most popular and representative play, The Little Foxes, revolves around the machinations of two Southern aristocratic families—the Hubbards and the Giddenses—who are the profiteers of post–Civil War reconstruction. Conflicts steadily build as Regina Giddens allies herself with her corrupt brothers, Ben and Oscar Hubbard, while detaching herself from her scrupulous husband, Horace, whom she no longer loves, and their daughter Alexandra, whose personal happiness has been gradually compromised by her opportunistic mother. A series of calculated reversals, including Horace's onstage death by stroke, underscores Hellman's theme of corruption and the struggle for power between good and evil characters.

Hellman's "well-made" play, with its sharply delineated character types, by no means suggests that she has intentionally succumbed to a patriarchal formula, despite the fact that this particular play, as well as several others of hers, demonstrates a negative model for any so-called women's theatre. Perhaps it is irrelevant that the protagonist, Regina Giddens, is a villainous woman who possesses not a single redeeming value, even if, at the play's conclusion, there is some implication that her daughter Alexandra has caught on to her scheming nature. It would also be chauvinistic to suggest that as a woman Hellman should have approached her central character more tactfully. What Hellman reveals is that the literary accomplishments of female playwrights are not always distinguishable from their male counterparts, a phenomenon that is more than likely the result of Western culture's influence on all writers, both male and female, until the middle of the twentieth century. Thereafter a heightened feminist movement "raised consciousness" in America, altering the course of aesthetics forever.

What Is Feminist Theatre?

In its broadest context feminist theatre is a thematic response to sociological and pyschological issues, namely, those that pertain to the welfare of women. With this altered perspective high on her list of priorities, playwright Ntozake Shange confronts its challenges in her choreopoem/drama, *for colored girls who have considered suicide / when the rainbow is enuf* (1976). Shange's achievement is threefold: (1) she has designed a dramatic structure that responds sensitively and uncomprisingly to her needs as a playwright and woman; (2) she has found a poetic language that reflects the interior lives of her seven black female characters; and (3) she explores a powerful theme—the instinct for survival—that achieves a universal appeal while addressing a specific female audience.

The form and content of Shange's aesthetic, which sharply disconnects from traditional structures, are not easily categorized. An aspect of this is effectively demonstrated in her handling of language—a "jazzy" and innovative verse style that is consistently uninhibited, rhythmic, and visually telegraphic. At one point, the "lady in blue" exclaims:

> ola
> my papa thot he was puerto rican & we wda been
> cept we waz just reglar niggahs wit hints of spanish
> so off i made it to this 36 hour marathon dance
> con salsa con ricardo
> 'suggggggggggar' ray on southern blvd
> next door to this fotografi place
> jammed wit burial weddin and communion relics
> next door to la real ideal genuine spanish barber
>   up up up up up stairs and stairs & lotsa hallway
> wit my colored new jersey self
> didn't know what anybody was saying
> cept if dancin was proof of origin
>   i was jibarita herself that nite
> & the next day

Shange's literary script grows out of a "collective theatre" process: the collaborative efforts of playwright, director, and actors to fashion a personal dramatic statement and performance piece. Constructed of more than twenty poems but viewed as a single statement—a form of verse drama to which Shange affixes the unique label of choreopoem— the script is divided among seven female performers who mirror the realities of seven kinds of women. Identified by the different colors of their dresses (e.g., "lady in purple," "lady in blue," as well as green, yellow, orange, red, and brown), the anonymous characters converse, soliloquize, sing, and dance a variety of experiences that celebrate their womanhood. Shange's rich and colorful idiom transforms each of these seven profiles into a three-dimensional character, each sharply contrasted from the other, until all contribute to a single collective consciousness in the formation of a human rainbow. Not coincidentally, the rainbow reflects the colors in a bruise's healing cycle—the central metaphor or image of the choreopoem.

How valid is Shange's aesthetic? Does it reflect the influences of our previous models yet retain its feminist identity? In point of fact, can we truly establish that Shange has made a conscious attempt to innovate a feminist model? Set on an empty stage, in a narrative format that conveniently allows the characters to confront us as well as their "sisters," there is an economy of theatrical effect that is unquestionably Brechtian. On the other hand, while the accumulative pattern of rising and falling actions lacks a clear Aristotelian design, Shange's emotional language provides a vivid landscape from which the interior lives of these women emerge, and it suggests a deliberately dramatic orientation. As a playwright, Shange incorporates both past and contemporary dramatic styles we have previously discussed, while remaining sensitive to the sexual politics that have fashioned her own selfhood.

Churchill's Radical Model

While Shange's lyrical view of "sisterhood" echoes one aspect of the concerns of contemporary women writers, British playwright Caryl Churchill addresses other aspects of feminism in a voice that is unrelentingly angry and a style that is strikingly realistic. In *Top Girls*, Churchill's seven women, though less anonymous than Shange's seven "ladies," also represent the varieties of womanhood. At a large banquet table, the narrator-like, contemporary protagonist Marlene hosts a party for some unusual guests, whom she proceeds to introduce to Griselda, the last guest to arrive:

> This is Joan who was Pope in the ninth century, and Isabella Bird, the Victorian Traveller, and Lady Nijo from Japan, Emperor's concubine and Buddhist nun, thirteenth century, nearer your own time, and Gret who was painted by Breughel.

Griselda's in Boccaccio and Petrarch and Chaucer because of her extraordinary marriage.

The didactic and matter-of-fact tone of Marlene's introduction complements Churchill's unique premise, in which the participation of numerous historical heroines, whose dinner-party conversation constitutes an important part of the play, reveals their joys and atrocities and, ironically, shows them to be a far cry from the "top girls" of the play's title. Having established this imaginative moment in theatrical time, Churchill abruptly shifts her locales to the Top Girls Employment Agency, where Marlene presides as owner, and the home of Marlene's working-class sister Joyce, whose teenage daughter, Angie, is really Marlene's illegitimate child, left to Joyce's care years earlier. In the final scene of the play, which takes place "a year earlier" than the previous scenes, Joyce confronts Marlene. (In reading the character dialogue, the playwright stipulates that "when one character starts speaking before the other has finished, the point of interruption is marked /."):

J: I don't know how you could leave your own child.

M: You were quick enough to take her.

J: Or what? Have her put in a home? Have some stranger / take her would you rather?

M: You couldn't have one so you took mine.

J: I didn't know that then.

M: Like hell, / married three years.

J: I didn't know that. Plenty of people / take that long.

M: Well it turned out lucky for you, didn't it?

J: Turned out all right for you by the look of you. You'd be getting a few less thousand a year.

M: Not necessarily.

J: You'd be stuck here / like you said.

M: I could have taken her with me.

J: You didn't want to take her with you. It's no good coming back now, Marlene, / and saying—

M: I know a managing director who's got two children, she breast feeds in the board room, she pays a thousand pounds a week on domestic help alone and she can afford

that because she's an extremely high-powered lady earning
a great deal of money.

With overlapping dialogue that allows both women to express what has
long been left unspoken, Marlene finally exposes the image of the
"extremely high-powered lady" she herself has failed to become. It is a
predicament that has made her professional behavior and personal
anger resemble those abusive, power-controlling men from whom she
once sought refuge. In addressing the issues of feminism and socialism,
Churchill's protagonist personifies the effects of poverty, wealth, and
power on the contemporary British woman. The sad effect is described
by the last word of the play, when Marlene confronts Angie who has
been awakened by a bad dream:

> Marlene: Did you have a bad dream? What happened in it?
> Well you're awake now, aren't you, pet?
>
> Angie: Frightening.

It is an open-ended conclusion, not unlike the terrifying reality that
Brecht's Shen Te confronted, and suggests a new beginning the
playwright asks us to build on.

Drawing Some Possible Conclusions

As long as a viable feminist aesthetic or model for the drama
continues to define itself, the literary results will give us, the playreaders, more to assess. In the meantime, if a work may be properly judged
according to its form and content, the plays of Hellman, Shange, and
Churchill reflect the pre- and postfeminist consciousness within and
outside America. As concerned playreaders, we are obligated: (1) to
view the female protagonists of any given historical period of the drama
in relation to prior existing character types created by men and women
playwrights; (2) to explore the ramifications of characters and themes,
especially those written by women, before and after the consciousness
raising of the latter half of the present century; (3) to assess the
theatricality of reputable plays written by women, separating the
one-dimensional social tracts from those viable plays that can capably
withstand a feminist interpretation; and (4) to recognize, once and for

all, that a contemporary feminist aesthetic must incorporate some depiction of what life is like for women who have been liberated from traditional roles.

Themes for Analysis: Dramatic Structures

In our preceding discussion, the subject of dramatic structures has encompassed a variety of issues, all of which can be amply demonstrated by carefully selected plays. In return, our specific reference to components within these plays should strengthen our understanding and enhance our discussion. Despite a categorical approach to the areas listed below, our approach to writing about individual dramatic structures may require an integrated view of several. For example, a discussion of Aristotelian structure may well incorporate the uses of dramatic irony. On the other hand, a study of the eclectic model is nearly impossible without some reference to the Brechtian structure. What matters is that we first recognize the separate issues involved in the study of dramatic structures before we integrate them for our own purposes of discussion. There are numerous areas to choose from, as reflected in the following topics:

Analogous Actions and Subplots

1. "The Use of Analogous Actions in Shakespeare's *King Lear.*"

2. "Shakespeare's Handling of Subplots in *A Midsummer Night's Dream.*"

3. The Trilogy Format of Aeschylus's *Oresteia.*"

4. "The Play-within-a-Play Structure of Pirandello's *Six Characters in Search of An Author.*"

5. "Why Minor Actions Are Major in Chekhov's *Three Sisters.*"

Dramatic Irony

1. "The Uses of Dramatic Irony in Shakespeare's *Othello.*"

2. "Tragic Irony in O'Neill's *Desire under the Elms.*"

3. "Stage Life After Death in Rabe's *Basic Training of Pavlo Hummel.*"

4. "The Comical Ironies of Character Relationships in Shaw's *Arms and the Man.*"

5. "Knowing More Than the Characters Know in Orton's *Loot.*"

Aristotelian Structure

1. "Complication and Recognition in Sophocles's *Oedipus Rex.*"

2. "Why Nothing Ever Happens in Beckett's *Waiting for Godot.*"

3. "How Shange's *for colored girls* Ignores the Rules."

4. "Hellman's *Little Foxes* as a Well-Made Play."

5. "Treatment of Time, Place, and Action in O'Neill's *Long Day's Journey Into Night.*"

Brechtian Structure

1. "Brecht Obeys His Own Rules in *Good Woman of Setzuan.*"

2. "The Brechtian Style of Shepard's *Tooth of Crime.*"

3. "Why Shaffer's *Equus* Fulfills the Brechtian Thesis."

4. "Sociopolitical Themes and Brechtian Structure in Churchill's *Top Girls.*"

5. "Evaluating Aristotelian versus Brechtian Structures in Selected Plays."

The Eclectic Model

1. "Identifying Artaudian and Brechtian Elements in Weiss's *Marat/Sade*."

2. "Ritual and Ceremony at the Center of Beck and Malina's *Paradise Now*."

3. "Rebuilding the Fourth Wall versus Alternative Theatre."

4. "Analyzing the Eclectic Ingredients in the Open Theatre's Production of *The Serpent*."

5. "How Certain Plays Support a Feminist Aesthetic."

Stage Conventions

1. "How the Character of the Porter Provides Comic Relief in Shakespeare's *Macbeth*."

2. "Examples of the Deus ex Machina in Television Sitcoms."

3. "Euripides's Handling of Medea's Fate."

4. "Tension versus Relief in Chekhov's *Cherry Orchard*."

5. "The Role of Fate versus the Need for Manipulation in Selected Plays."

CHAPTER SIX
LANGUAGE: THE KEY TO
CHARACTER AND ACTION

Sweet smoke of rhetoric!
—*Love's Labour's Lost*, III, i

As Shakespeare's Armado rapturously exclaims, the playwright's "burning" language provides us with the most dependable clues to understanding the internal motives and external behaviors of his characters. Language specifically refers to dialogue, suggesting that our concern for scenic and character descriptions (certainly vital aspects of the play's effectiveness) must be evaluated apart from its spoken messages, which hold priority. This would stand to reason, since a play is written *to be spoken by characters onstage,* despite the existence of certain "closet dramas," a select category of literary plays deemed unworthy or incapable of stage production that find life *only* on the printed page. In this respect, the playwright's language must be suitably versatile to capture the attention of both listener (in the theatre) and playreader (in his study). For both respondents, however, the function of language is threefold: (1) to cement character relationships; (2) to convey rational verbal and nonverbal message units; and (3) to strengthen our grasp of the stage actions unfolding before us. Thus, while we need to hear these characters (the importance of which has been reinforced in an earlier discussion), it is equally important that we understand them.

The undeniable permanence of language encompasses a variety of cadences, tones, linguistic components, meanings, and purposes. Classical conventions have already demonstrated that the language of verse should appropriately serve the tragic form—a somewhat rigid characteristic that sat comfortably with Shakespeare and his contemporaries as well as their predecessors. Yet Shakespeare applied the rhythmic cadence of iambic pentameter to all of his plays, achieving entirely different ends through a range of effects and mastering consistently lively conversational tones, in a style we ultimately label "poetic." At the other end of our spectrum is the realistic style of prose, a less heightened and artificial language that sought to mirror modern characters in an age that showed less concern for formal tragedy than it did for melodrama, or what would become popularly known as "serious drama." What remains absolutely vital to all of these uses of language, ranging from the classical Greeks to the contemporary absurdists, are those essential literary techniques that heighten the dimensions of language and allow it not just to state but to illuminate. In our cumulative view of language as a key to character and action, we will deliberately avoid a chronological patterning and assess its illuminations whenever, as in the theatre, selected fragments of character dialogue assault our playreading imaginations.

Language as Subtext

In Sam Shepard's *Buried Child* (1978), we are introduced to a contemporary family. The setting is a sparsely furnished living room. The father, named Dodge, slyly gulps from a whiskey bottle as he sits before the flickering light of a silent TV set. He converses with his wife, Halie, who remains unseen at the top of the living room staircase. Their oldest son Tilden appears with ears of corn piled in his arms. He stares at his father and then walks slowly to him and dumps the corn in his lap. After a "long pause" indicated by the playwright, a deceptively simple exchange occurs:

> Dodge: Are you having trouble here, Tilden! Are you in some kind of trouble?
>
> Tilden: I'm not in any trouble.
>
> Dodge: You can tell me if you are. I'm still your father.
>
> Tilden: I know you're still my father.
>
> Dodge: I know you had a little trouble back in New Mexico. That's why you came out here.
>
> Tilden: I never had any trouble.
>
> Dodge: Tilden, your mother told me all about it.
>
> Tilden: What'd she tell you?

(Tilden pulls some chewing tobacco out of his jacket and bites off a plug.)

Dodge: I don't have to repeat what she told me! She told me all about it!

Tilden: Can I bring my chair in from the kitchen?
Dodge: What?
Tilden: Can I bring my chair from the kitchen?
Dodge: Sure. Bring your chair in.

The unanswered questions suggested by this interaction transform its vaguely familiar realistic setting into a *surreal* or irrational landscape of the emotions, filled with moral and psychological implications, which, like hidden motifs, constitute the *subtext* of the play. Beyond a mere reading of the dialogue, the playreader's task is to decode the *iconography*, or vocabulary of visual images and verbal "impressions," that Shepard uses to illuminate his dramatic purpose.

Aside from the household setting, which is itself a *microcosm*, or miniature reflection, of some chaotic wilderness, the geographic locale is anonymous. The silent TV set, accompanied by a talkative but unseen Halie, suggests that the communication network between husband and wife has disintegrated—a popular theme in the American drama. Furthermore, alcohol affects Dodge's perception of the world and quite possibly his verbal responses to it. Now the appearance of Tilden, weighed down with unhusked corn—a reliable American farm product and possible symbol in this stage action—suggests a midwestern locale. Up to this point, however, we must rely on guess work, for Shepard intends that both father and son, preparing to converse, should offer us few clues about their ambiguous relationship. This is further compounded by the fact—withheld from us at this point of the action—that Dodge's farm has been barren for decades.

So we are left with no alternative but to decipher both verbal and nonverbal evidence. Perhaps Tilden represents the prodigal son, returning with gifts to appease an angry father. Is this allusion, or reference, to the New Testament deliberate? Does it clarify this "trouble" that Dodge seems to know about, through Halie, but Tilden denies? Dodge does not want "to repeat what she told me" yet forces Tilden to repeat his request for a chair from the kitchen. This verbal exchange, built on staccato-like rhythms, cautiously communicates its message to us through repetition and *indirection*, that is, by purposely avoiding *specific* reference. A careful rereading of the exchange exposes the rhythmical repetition of identical key words shared between father and son, points to their deceptively retarded level of communication, and finally reinforces its dark humor and remoteness. A cautious and imaginative playreader soon realizes that this simple but strangely inarticulate conversation not only *foreshadows* further compelling interactions, but reflects Shepard's serious concerns with language and family relationships.

Achieving a Poetry *of* the Theatre

Having sampled the verbal iconography of Shepard's world, let us consider the contrasting relationship of another father and son who have reached a point of total confrontation in exposing their long-kept secrets. There is no need of subtext or stage props in the fourth and final act of O'Neill's *Long Day's Journey into Night* (1956), when James Tyrone, once a famous stage actor, has just confessed some of the more personal moments of his life to his younger son, Edmund. In return, Edmund decides to share some of his experiences that pertain directly to the sea.

> Edmund: . . . the moment of ecstatic freedom came. The peace, the end of the quest, the last harbor, the joy of belonging to a fulfillment beyond men's lousy, pitiful, greedy fears and hopes and dreams! And several other times in my life, when I was swimming far out, or lying alone on the beach, I have had the same experience. Became the sun, the hot sand, green seaweed anchored to a rock, swaying in the tide. Like a saint's vision of beatitude. Like the veil of things as they seem drawn back by an unseen hand. For a second you see—and seeing the secret, are the secret. For a second there is meaning. Then the hand lets the veil fall and you are alone, lost in the fog again, and you stumble on toward nowhere, for no good reason. It was a great mistake, my being born a man, I would have been much more successful as a seagull or a fish. As it is, I will always be a stranger who never feels at home, who does not really want and is not really wanted, who can never belong, who must always be a little in love with death!

> Tyrone: Yes, there's the makings of a poet in you all right. But that's morbid craziness about not being wanted and loving death.

Edmund: The *makings* of a poet. No, I'm afraid I'm like the guy who is always panhandling for a smoke. He hasn't even got the makings. He's got only the habit. I couldn't touch what I tried to tell you just now. I just stammered. That's the best I'll ever do. I mean, if I live. Well, it will be faithful realism, at least. Stammering is the native eloquence of us fog people.

In this admittedly autobiographical play, O'Neill achieves a clarity and effortlessness of expression that matches the ecstatic abandon Edmund feels towards the sea. Edmund's reverie tells us he is a dreamer easily given to introspection, who has lived his young life with great passion. But his self-description also discloses a sadness at the realization that he cannot *belong*, a motif voiced by other O'Neill characters. Now Tyrone pays his son the only compliment of the play when he tells him he has the "makings of a poet." Edmund has always dreamed of becoming a writer, but his ode to life is evenly matched by a morbid preoccupation with death, a preoccupation heightened by a fear expressed earlier in the play—that his "summer cold" may be more serious than he wants to believe. In portraying the tragic mood of this as well as the other doomed characters of the play, O'Neill's vivid prose achieves a certain *poetry of the theatre:* a heightened and sustained emotional expression, often the domain of poetry, that reveals the soul's darker conflicts.

The confessional tone of this passage becomes a microcosm of the whole play and, despite Edmund's "faithful realism," finds appropriate lyrical expression in the flowing cadences of a prose style that contrasts sharply with Shepard's minimalism. Employing a verbal iconography so ripe with sea imagery, O'Neill eloquently introduces the symbols of "fish," "fog," "sea gull," and "seaweed" to integrate his tragic young protagonist with the forces of nature and make him regret having been "born a man." In his flexible handling of realistic language, these symbolic references allow O'Neill, like Shepard, to extend his message beyond a literal or specific level of meaning, to a more heightened, poetic expression, aptly described as "the native eloquence of us fog people." But the effect of such emotional "stammering," as Edmund cynically calls it, is quite the opposite of Shepard's: it functions to conjoin father and son; it opens, rather than frustrates, the communication between them.

The Uses of Dramatic Irony

Our assessment of the language in Aeschylus discloses a very different domestic setting and communication flow from our preceding examples. Whereas O'Neill achieves certain poetic effects through a natural prose style, Aeschylus's deliberate verse structure—an example of the use of poetry *in* the theatre—incorporates a variety of poetic devices, adheres to the conventions of the theatre for which it was written, and ennobles the royal cast of characters who speak it. In *Agamemnon*, the first play of Aeschylus's trilogy, *The Oresteia* (458 B.C.), the Chorus of Argive elders welcomes its victorious King Agamemnon, suddenly returned from battle. Notice how the austere language and formidable tone of the Chorus's monologue—spoken as one character but experienced on a more massive choral scale—builds toward a complexity of factual detail, psychological insight, and tragic foreshadowing:

> Welcome, great King, stormer of Troy,
> True son of Atreus.
> How shall I greet you? How shall I honor you?
> Not overstepping, not underscoring
> The appropriate praises.
> Too many people favor appearances
> And offend what is right.
> Everyone's ready to sigh for the stricken,
> But the pang and the sorrow
> Never goes through to the heart.
> Show them rejoicers: they take on rejoicing,
> Forcing their faces to smile.
> But the good shepherd knows his sheep
> And never mistakes the eyes of a man
> Who is fraud when he seems to be friend
> And cheats with his watery fondness.
>
> Even you—let me tell you—equipping your army
> Hot after Helen, for me were depicted
> Once in very poor colors:
> Not steering aright your rudder of reason;
> Conjuring up courage for men who were dying,
> By the blood of a sacrifice.

But now from my heart not lightly nor loveless,
"Welcome!" I say on work well done.
In the course of time you will learn by inquiring
Which were honest ones, which were dishonorable
Citizens guarding the city.

What does this message tell us? That Agamemnon must not be deceived by appearances; that a good shepherd "knows his sheep / And never mistakes the eyes of a man / Who is fraud when he seems to be friend." The clever analogy—just one of several clues—warns Agamemnon that Aegisthus, who appears to be a friend, is not. The language contains sufficient *dramatic irony* to reveal to us more than Agamemnon himself perceives: that Aegisthus is the lover of Agamemnon's wife, Clytemnestra; that Clytemnestra's adulterous behavior has been partially motivated to get revenge on a husband who sacrificed their daughter, Iphigenia, to the gods, in exchange for fair sailing winds to Troy; that deception, not honesty, will soon greet this heroic king now returned home. The destructive hereditary curse on the House of Atreus is about to be set into motion. The grandest irony of all is the Chorus's prophetic language, in itself a formal and rigid microcosm that tells Agamemnon nothing less than the truth but cannot save his life.

Having grasped the content, we reconsider the form in which it is revealed. Riding with the rhythm of a bold and declamatory verse style that captures the Chorus's warnings, we recognize the very clues Agamemnon is fated to ignore. In Paul Roche's embellished translation from the Greek, Aeschylus's language remains simple and direct, allowing the Chorus to know its rightful place but also to "personalize" when called on to do so, as when it suddenly reprimands Agamemnon's behavior "depicted / Once in very poor colors." Such language, accompanied by a built-in authoritative tone, allows the Chorus to fulfill its function as principal narrator of events and "conscience" to the protagonist.

There are, however, numerous unpredictable ingredients to the Chorus's mode of expression. We notice how the balanced construction of the opening interrogatives: "How shall I greet you? How shall I honor you?" is counterpointed by the semi-alliterative echoes: "Not overstepping, not underscoring / The appropriate praises." Or its graceful, short alliteratives—"sigh for the stricken" and "forcing their faces to smile"— to describe those among us who are easily deceived. Appropriately adhering to a seafaring vocabulary that is strengthened by alliteration, the chorus condemns the awkward steering of Agamemnon's "rudder of reason" but counteracts its attack with an apology from a heart that speaks "not lightly nor loveless." We are ultimately moved by the message's poetic language, suspenseful content, and, above all, dramatic irony, all of which inform *us*, rather than Agamemnon, of his fatal homecoming.

Wordplay, Double-Entendre, and the Language of Comedy

The formality of Aeschylus's verse is loosened by the iambic pentameter of Shakespeare's *comic language* in *The Taming of the Shrew* (1594). In the following confrontation, notice how Katharine and Petruchio achieve a realistic conversational tone in spite of the carefully measured, five-beat metrical lines that characterize their verbal dueling. (In the opening six lines, including two metrical lines shared by both characters, the boldfacing of each of the five stressed or accented syllables should facilitate our awareness of Shakespeare's use of the iambic pentameter structure and its semblance to conversational speech patterns. Its contribution to the meaning of Shakespeare's language is undeniable.) When Petruchio announces he has been moved to woo Katharine for his wife, her response is immediate:

K: **Moved?** In good **time.** Let **him** that **moved** you **hith**er
   Remove you **hence;** I **knew** you at the **first.**
   You were a **move**able.

P: **Why, what's** a **move**able?

K: A **joint-stool.**

P: **Thou** hast **hit** it. Come **sit** on me.

K: **Asses** are **made** to **bear,** and **so** are **you.**

P: **Women** are **made** to **bear,** and **so** are **you.**

K: No such jade as you, if me you mean.

P: Alas good Kate, I will not burden thee.
   For knowing thee to be young and light—

K: Too light for such a swain as you to catch,
   And yet as heavy as my weight should be.

P: Should be? Should—buzz!

K: Well taken, and like a buzzard.

P: O slow-winged turtle, shall a buzzard take thee?

K: Ay, for a turtle, as he takes a buzzard.

P: Come, come, you wasp, in faith you are too angry.

K: If I be waspish, best beware my sting.

This rapid-fire exchange, or *stichomythia*, characterizes one of the funniest seduction scenes of all English comedy. Once its tone and tempo have been established, Shakespeare's language grows dangerously playful as it first conceals, then reveals, elements of humor, sexual banter, and romance.

The comic tone is animated by imaginative wordplay: "moved," "move," "remove," "moveable," "joint-stool," "come sit on me." A series of related sounds conveys meaning to the listener and, above all, provides important visual clues to the playreader, who soon discovers that Petruchio has found the surest way to grab Katharine in his arms, then pull her onto his lap. At closer inspection, fine-tuned wordplay turns into *punning* when, all at once, the "burden" that Petruchio imposes on their conversation turns insultingly to Katharine's weight. The physical entanglements, revealed through the wordplay of both characters, tease our imagination.

But such wordplay also reflects a syncopation and connectedness, allowing each character to toss out an image that is instantly retrieved and embellished by the other. If Petruchio has been "moved to woo," Katharine retorts that he "remove" himself hence. Her assertion that "asses are made to bear" meets his identical response about women. Even his teasingly aimed "buzz" boomerangs as "buzzard," thanks to her quick-tongued aggression. But when Petruchio finally counterattacks by calling her a wasp, she sharply cautions him to "beware [her] sting." Insult is followed by injury, while witty wordplay leads to sexual implication, only to explode in a knockabout brawl. Shakespeare's language serves to highlight the comical impact of their relationship, to let them confront us on a singularly verbal level. We gradually surmise that the shrewish Katharine is not quite clever enough to escape from Petruchio's "taming"—a predicament repeated throughout a play in which language has served as the key to an ongoing battle between the sexes.

The Art of Rhyming Couplets

One stylistic variation of verse drama and an attribute of its versatility is the use of *rhymed couplets*, as manifested in the comedies of Moliere. Using a tighter rhyme scheme than that of Shakespeare, yet conforming to the popular iambic pentameter, the French playwright constructs a verse pattern in which individual pairs of poetic lines terminate with the identical sound and create a heightened rhyming effect. (The underlining of the first two pairs, below, should help us recognize them.) In his translations of Moliere's plays, the American poet Richard Wilbur has chosen to retain the original metrical pattern as well as the striking rhymed couplets that highlight each of the verse pairings. With effects that seem far from conversational in tone and tempo, the results prove challenging and pleasurable to our playreading sensibilities, as demonstrated in this passage from *Tartuffe* (1664), in which the unsavory title character—a two-faced religious mentor by day who is transformed into a playboy at night—attempts to seduce the wife of the man who employs him for spiritual guidance:

> Madam, forget such fears, and be my <u>pupil,</u>
> And I shall teach you how to conquer <u>scruple.</u>
> Some joys, it's true, are wrong in Heaven's <u>eyes;</u>
> Yet Heaven is not averse to <u>compromise;</u>
> There is a science, lately formulated,
> Whereby one's conscience may be liberated,
> And any wrongful act you care to mention
> May be redeemed by purity of intention.
> I'll teach you, Madam, the secrets of that science;
> Meanwhile, just place on me your full reliance.
> Assuage my keen desires, and feel no dread:
> The sin, if any, shall be on my head.

Indeed, Tartuffe's proposal is most persuasive, revealing a smooth control of language in which he flamboyantly luxuriates, while guarding his perverse and hypocritical nature. By retaining the form and spirit of Moliere's original, which other translators have rendered into unimaginative prose, Wilbur deliberately draws us into the carefully worded content of Tartuffe's message and lets the six pairs of rhymed couplets playfully distract our reading and listening attention—all to serve the attention-getting theatrical effort Moliere intended. In short, the *form* of the verse matches the cleverness of its *content,* as both playwright and translator remain sensitive to our playreading instincts and reveal newer depths in the verse format.

Elitist Prose and the Comedy of Manners

The flashy humor and physical interplay suggested through Shakespeare's conversational verse and the smoother, more rounded tones of Moliere's rhymes are transformed into a more intellectual prose exercise by two contrasting conversationalists—the beautiful Millamant and her suitor, Mirabell, in Congreve's *Way of the World*. So civilized and amorally independent are both speakers that in the single scene in which they are alone together they mutually devise a marital contract in which the elaborate wording proves as provocative as its content. Their language is a fashionable prose that is no less attention-getting than Moliere's "well-spoken" verse. Millamant is clearly the more insistent, as she proclaims her "will and pleasure" to Mirabell:

> Mill: I won't be called names after I'm married; positively I won't be called names.
>
> Mir: Names!
>
> Mill: Ay, as wife, spouse, my dear, joy, jewel, love, sweetheart, and the rest of that nauseous cant, in which men and their wives are so fulsomely familiar—I shall never bear that—good Mirabell, don't let us be familiar or fond, nor kiss before folks, like my Lady Fadler and Sir Francis: nor go to Hyde-park together the first Sunday in a new chariot, to provoke eyes and whispers, and then never to be seen there together again; as if we were proud of one another the first week, and ashamed of one another ever after. Let us never visit together, nor go to a play together; but let us be very strange and well-bred: let us be as strange as if we had been married a great while; and as well-bred as if we were not married at all.

Millamant's smooth, legato-like declaration, characterized by a delicately chosen vocabulary, demonstrates a technical virtuosity, rare in prose dialogue, that epitomizes the Restoration style. We perceive her words and images as they vividly conjure up the more prominent activities of the upperclass: lovemaking, playgoing, and promenading in the park. Above all, they reveal Millamant as a woman of importance, one who sets herself apart from the ordinary and who refuses to perpetuate the "nauseous cant" that commonly characterizes her rank and class. In a message devoid of subtext, wordplay, and symbolic repercussion, Millamant minces no words in declaring her position sharply and wittily to Mirabell.

Unlike Katharine, who must physically strategize her relationship with Petruchio, Millamant never budges. Her strength stems from a verbal agility and an unbending constitution, although Congreve allows her several graceful strokes at alliteration—for example, "joy, jewel," "fulsomely familiar," "familiar or fond," and "like my Lady Fadler"—which enhance her message and capture our attention. Such lyrical prose suggests a sensitive side to Millamant's forthrightness, despite a summing up in which she transforms two dissimilar word choices—"strange" and "well-bred"—into coldly compatible and sensible logic.

Her demands seem endless. When Mirabell asks her if she has "any more conditions to offer," she continues with a list of *infinitive statements*—a grand total of ten—detailing what she will do when married:

> to pay and receive visits to and from whom I please; to write and receive letters, without interrogatories or wry faces on your part; to wear what I please; and choose conversation with regard only to my own taste . . . to be sole empress of my tea-table, which you must never presume to approach without first asking leave . . .

And so her demands continue. With the finality of a death sentence, in a tone of jaded sophistication, she urges Mirabell's adherence to these terms before she will allow herself to "dwindle into a wife."

Mirabell's response is a match for Millamant's, pointing to an agenda of equally detailed, eloquently stated "provisos" which must be agreed on before he, in turn, may prove a "tractable and complying husband." But the seriousness of his tone is humorously betrayed by the frivolity of its content, for example, as he discloses one of his more vehement demands:

> I denounce against all strait lacing, squeezing for a shape, till you mould my boy's head like a sugar-loaf, and instead of a man child, make me father to a crooked billet. Lastly, to the dominion of the tea-table I submit—but with proviso, that you exceed not in your

province; but restrain yourself to native and simple tea-table drinks . . . and tea-table talk.

While there is an unexpected contemporaneity in Mirabell's attack on women's fashions, there is a firm implication that fatherhood is at the center of his concerns. When Millamant finally exclaims, "I hate your odious provisos," Mirabell quickly responds, "Then we are agreed!" and, kissing her hand, seals their contract for a match not exactly made in heaven.

We admire the precision of Congreve's words spoken by characters like Millamant and Mirabell. He uses a vocabulary that elicits our laughter while provoking our thoughts on the serious subject of marriage and relationships; he makes use of a tightly structured grammatical style that is perfectly suited to their Restoration temperaments. However, such language is more than a matter of form or a glittering facade devoid of content. Proving to us, once and for all, that prose dialogue need not be prosaic, Congreve's style endures because his characters need words to survive, to assert themselves with humor, and to rise triumphantly above their less literate counterparts who, lacking this dispassionate verbal agility, are defenseless.

Didacticism and Medieval Character Dialogue

After encountering the worldlier characters and ornate language of Shakespeare, Congreve, or even Moliere, and the weightier prose styles of O'Neill and Shepard, it might seem ill-timed to turn abruptly to the language of the late Middle English period. Nevertheless, the language of medieval drama reveals a simplicity, directness, and austerity seldom achieved on the stages of England and Western Europe, so for the sake of exploring these unique contrasts alone, its values remain essential to our study of language in the drama. A brief recollection of medieval stage history should enable us to link its drama to the church and recognize once again the didactic ends that language served. Since we have already observed the central figure of Everyman surrounded by his supporting cast in an earlier part of our study, let us now approach their dialogue as a key to character and action and as a microcosm of the anonymous medieval playwright's achievement.

In the concluding scene from the *Everyman* morality play (1500), the eponymous character finds himself abandoned by Beauty, Strength,

Discretion, and Five Wits. In desperation, he addresses Good Deeds and Knowledge, who still remain at his side:

> Everyman: O Iesu, help! All hath forsaken me!
>
> Good Deeds: Nay, Everyman; I wyll byde with thee.
> I wyll not forsake thee indede;
> Thou shalte fynde me a good frende at nede.
>
> Everyman: Gramercy, Good Dedes!
> Now may I true frendes see.
> They have forsaken me, everyone;
> I loved them better than my Good Dedes alone.
> Knowledge, will ye forsake me also?
>
> Knowledge: Ye, Everyman, whan ye to Deth shall go;
> But not yet, for no maner of daunger.
>
> Everyman: Gramercy, Knowledge, with all my herte!
>
> Knowledge: Nay, yet I wyll not from hens departe
> Tyll I see where ye shall be come.
>
> Everyman: Methynke, alas, that I must be gone
> To make my rekenynge, and my dettes paye;
> For I see my tyme is nye spent awaye.
> Take example, all ye that this do here or see,
> How they that I loved best do forsake me,
> Excepte my Good Dedes that bydeth truely.

We cannot overlook the simple, yet powerful message that is communicated through Everyman's words, a familiar moral lesson taught to the audience for whom it was originally written and enacted. By now we are prepared to look beyond its one-dimensional tone and purpose, however, and grasp the subtleties lying beneath its uncluttered surface. Perhaps we sense the poignancy of Everyman's desperation as he confronts his last hour with only his "good deeds" to rest on. A final discovery that cherished "knowledge" is just a fleeting friend who will soon abandon him represents the turning point at which he must exit alone. Yet he does this with a nobility and courage gently captured in a simple verse structure that remains subordinate to its eloquent message.

At the top of the passage, for example, Everyman's "me" is matched by Good Deeds's "thee," to link the two characters through rhyme. Their exchange is further balanced when Good Deeds' "nede" (need) counterpoints Everyman's "dedes," while Everyman's "herte" (heart) is highlighted by Knowledge's "departe." With debts to "paye" and time spent "awaye," Everyman's rhyming response connects one last time with things physical (his debts) and earthly (time). Suddenly he asserts, in an outspoken three-line rhyme, his awareness that man is but the sum of his actions: the isolated *vertical* arrangement or versification of these rhyme words—"see," "me," "truely"—becomes an ironic disclosure or self-exposure, a kind of coded command and verbal stripping away, as if Everyman has come full circle and now asks us to recognize in him something about ourselves. No matter how much we might read into these clues, the joy of discovery outweighs the tendency to misinterpret and ultimately increases our playreading enjoyment. The anonymous author of *Everyman* confirms that there is more here than at first meets the eye.

Brevity, Subtlety, and Innuendo

While fathers and sons strive to understand each other, candid lovers confront their fate, and a noble Agamemnon and humble Everyman prepare for their final journeys, we are reminded that the variations of verbal confrontation are likely to happen wherever two or three characters convene and that the setting for such interaction, as we have already observed, is subordinate to the *psychological* center established by the language of the characters. This would suggest that if both characters and motives have been carefully drawn by the playwright, language will seem to occur spontaneously and effortlessly in any corner of the stage or page. It is in the living room, or rather the inevitable drawing room, its nineteenth-century counterpart, that Ibsen's men and women gather and thrive on sharp verbal exchanges, and the survival of the strongest is often painfully demonstrated through language. In *Hedda Gabler*, Jorgen Tesman, recently married to the beautiful Hedda Gabler and returned home after an extended honeymoon, greets his Aunt Juliane Tesman. After a short conversation, Hedda appears, and the following interaction occurs:

> Tesman: [*discovering his old bedroom slippers*] I can't tell you how I've missed them! Do have a look at them, Hedda—
>
> Hedda: I'm not very interested, Jorgen—
>
> Tesman: Dear Aunt Rima embroidered them for me during

her illness. They have so many memories for me—

Hedda: Scarcely for me, Jorgen.

Miss Tesman: Of course not, Jorgen! They mean nothing to Hedda.

Tesman: I only thought, now that she's one of the family—

Hedda: We shall never get on with this servant, Jorgen!

Miss Tesman: Not get on with Berte?

Tesman: Hedda dear, what do you mean?

Hedda: Look! She's left her old hat lying about on the table.

Tesman: Why, Hedda!

Hedda: Just imagine if someone were to come in and see it!

Tesman: But, Hedda! That's Aunt Juliane's hat!

Hedda: Oh! Is it?

Miss Tesman: Yes, indeed it is! And what's more it's not old—little Mrs. Tesman!

Hedda: I really didn't look at it very closely, Miss Tesman.

Miss Tesman: [*puts on the hat*] This is the very first time I've worn it!

Tesman: And it's a lovely hat, too—quite a beauty!

Miss Tesman: Oh, it isn't as beautiful as all that. Where's my parasol? Ah—here it is! For this is mine too— not Berte's.

Tesman: A new hat and a new parasol—just think, Hedda!

Hedda: Most handsome and lovely, I'm sure!

Tesman: Yes, isn't it, eh? But do take a good look at Hedda— see how lovely she is!

Miss Tesman: Hedda was always lovely, my dear boy—that's nothing new. [*She nods and prepares to leave.*]

This compact exchange demonstrates how vital messages can be communicated in the shortest, subtlest of strokes. Anticipating quieter lifts of intensity toward building this first act and preparing us for more explosive confrontations in the later acts, Ibsen deliberately conserves the energies of his characters by choosing to focus on smaller, more trivial details. The dialogue bursts with clues, however, all of which point to the predatory nature of Hedda Gabler. In failing to acknowledge her husband's newly embroidered slippers—a symbol of his gentle, domestic nature—she instantly rejects all he holds dear, including his two elderly aunts. Although Tesman hopes to welcome Hedda as "one of the family," it is clear that her proud, manipulative, and destructive remarks set her quite apart from these lesser characters. Instinctively, Miss Tesman perceives the loveless marriage her nephew has entered and, simply choosing to accept Hedda's insults, exits quietly.

Ibsen's straightforward, realistic prose style, accurately captured in Eva Le Gallienne's highly readable translation, carefully avoids poetic cadences, embellished word choices, and repetition—elements that have worked to great advantage in our earlier examples. Instead Ibsen achieves a language of *innuendo*, allowing gestures and words to insinuate, that is, to imply what is most derogatory. After all, why do we not accept Hedda's "mistaken" belief that the article of clothing belongs to their servant? Is Hedda infallible? Quite simply, we choose to interpret her reference to this "old hat lying about on the table" as protest as well as complaint, that such calculated wording is *her* way of greeting Tesman's aunt. She is exposed through innuendo, while her husband remains oblivious to her words and can only see "how lovely she is!" Hedda's excuse, that she "really didn't look at it very closely," is the coldest sort of apology, accepting the fact that the hat is indeed quite new and has not been worn previously. The scene's effectiveness is best demonstrated in the fact that Hedda reveals the depth of her heartless nature in fewer than eight short remarks, once again allowing Ibsen to confirm the power of prose.

Anti-Style and the Language of the Absurd

Ibsen's obsession with certain "truths" imparted through language is reminiscent of the "faithful realism" Edmund attributes to those unlucky "fog people," who must communicate through "stammering." Thus we, as playreaders, must evaluate the objectivity of stage language, whether it loosely recreates an incident from real life, as it often did for O'Neill, or merely rearranges the fabric of fiction, as it has popularly served most playwrights for centuries. That is why the dramatic assaults on language by the contemporary Rumanian playwright Eugene Ionesco have illuminated our preoccupation with words, including the tragic or hilarious predicaments from which they stem. Ionesco was previously acknowledged in our study as the principal forerunner of a theatre tradition called Theatre of the Absurd, where the manifestations of language are deeply connected to certain philosophical premises—namely, that mankind has lost its reason. His plays achieve a devaluation of language and imply no more than what their characters tell us. In Ionesco's long one-act play *The Bald Soprano*, we meet Mr. and Mrs. Martin, who have just discovered that they have indeed met before, are married to each other, and, furthermore, are the parents of a daughter named Alice. After their joyful reacquaintance, they are greeted by their hosts, Mr. and Mrs. Smith, who sit facing their guests, before speaking after "a long embarrassed silence":

> Mr. Smith: Hm. [*Silence.*]
>
> Mrs. Smith: Hm, hm. [*Silence.*]
>
> Mrs. Martin: Hm, hm, hm. [*Silence.*]
>
> Mr. Martin: Hm, hm, hm, hm. [*Silence.*]
>
> Mrs. Martin: Oh, but definitely. [*Silence.*]
>
> Mr. Martin: We all have colds. [*Silence.*]
>
> Mr. Smith: Nevertheless, it's not chilly. [*Silence.*]
>
> Mrs. Smith: There's no draft. [*Silence.*]
>
> Mr. Martin: Oh no, fortunately. [*Silence.*]
>
> Mr. Smith: Oh dear, oh dear, oh dear. [*Silence.*]
>
> Mr. Martin: Don't you feel well? [*Silence.*]
>
> Mrs. Smith: No, he's wet his pants. [*Silence.*]
>
> Mrs. Martin: Oh, sir, at your age, you shouldn't. [*Silence.*]
>
> Mr. Smith: The heart is ageless. [*Silence.*]
>
> Mr. Martin: That's true. [*Silence.*]
>
> Mrs. Smith: So they say. [*Silence.*]
>
> Mrs. Martin: They also say the opposite. [*Silence.*]
>
> Mr. Smith: The truth lies somewhere between the two.
>   [*Silence.*]
>
> Mr. Martin: That's true. [*Silence.*]

Before their dialogue disintegrates into well-chosen gibberish, meaningless nonsequiturs, and strings of vowels and consonants hurled hysterically at each other, Ionesco grants the Martins and the Smiths some brief opportunity to "make sense"—the primary task of language. Since the scene depicts a social visit, cluttered with the grunts and empty chatter we are acquainted with in our own real lives, the event is meaningful to its participants and approached with total seriousness. Except for the fact that Ionesco has been clever enough to "theatricalize" their speech behavior in his attempt to satirize the empty rituals of our everyday lives, his four-character dialogue often conveys the aura of an exercise and so risks sounding a bit simplistic to our more sophisticated expectations. Allowing that there are no hidden messages "between the lines," the Martins and the Smiths use language to reveal the funny and not-so-funny "games people play."

The attention-getting ritual, manifested here in the typical clearing of throats, turns into the game of one-upmanship as one "hm" is followed by two "hm"s and so forth. In the meantime, the nonverbal dramatic pauses feed into the increasing awkwardness and discomfort of a situation that has yet to define itself. This is followed by a blatant nonsequitur, as Mrs. Martin's "Oh, but definitely" precedes her husband's assertion about having "colds." The Martins mirror each other, or at least think in the same way, as some married people are prone to do, just as the Smiths respond in their mutual agreement that "it's not chilly" and "there's no draft." In other words, the game is called "subject closed" or "Shut Up!" When Mr. Smith wets his pants, demonstrating the behavior of a two-year-old, the name of the game is "Men Will Be Boys," until he *poeticizes* his behavior by announcing that "the heart is ageless." Since it is impolite to disagree with one's host, however, Mrs. Martin can only concur, before slyly interjecting that the opposite may also be true. Recognizing this as a "put-down," Mr. Smith calmly reconsiders that the truth rests "somewhere between the two," with which Mr. Martin politely agrees. Whether Ionesco is exploring the more profound areas of absurdity in the human condition, as Samuel Beckett has chosen to do, or is merely reveling in its lighter implications, the logical illogic of *The Bald Soprano* squarely addresses viable issues of language and meaning in the drama.

Solving the Riddles of Language

Our return to language in its more contemporary uses has been deliberately circular. Not that Shepard and Harold Printer reflect similar literary styles, which is not the case at all, but their characters would almost seem to inhabit a similar consciousness. It is not surprising, therefore, that Shepard's equally prolific playwright-contemporary, David Mamet, should dedicate his vitriolic *Glengarry Glen Ross* to Pinter, as if Mamet had also been inspired by Pinter's menacing characters and environments, not to mention the irrepressible language, both verbal and nonverbal, of the British playwright. (Perhaps a tip to the playreader is to make note of the play's dedication if there is one, then draw some possible conclusions!) It is not fair, however, to credit Pinter alone for exposing the raw nerve that may occasionally be felt underneath the literal surfaces of the plays of his contemporaries. Like Ionesco, with whom he shares some undeniable qualities, Pinter is a forerunner whose contribution to the theatricality of language remains incomparable. Whereas Ionesco's characters give "sound" to their observations, Pinter's characters "resound." For that matter, two Pinter characters, confronting each other in an empty room—the essential environment for Pinter's people—radiate a very different energy from the two Shepard characters who opened our observations on language. Yet both playwrights depend on language to reconstruct their characters' yet undefined relationships.

In the following dialogue from Pinter's *Homecoming* (1965), Ruth converses with her brother-in-law Lenny, whom she has met for the first time just moments earlier. They are alone in the family living room. Lenny, claiming to be sensitive to the unreasonable demands people make on him, has related a story to Ruth, when he abruptly stops to ask Ruth a question:

L: Excuse me, shall I take this ashtray out of your way?

R: It's not in my way.

L: It seems to be in the way of your glass. The glass was about to fall. Or the ashtray. I'm rather worried about the carpet. It's not me, it's my father. He's obsessed with order and clarity. He doesn't like a mess. So, as I don't believe you're smoking at the moment, I'm sure you won't object if I move the ashtray.

[*He does so.*]

And now perhaps I'll relieve you of your glass.

R: I haven't quite finished.

L: You've consumed quite enough, in my opinion.

R: No, I haven't.

L: Quite sufficient, in my opinion.

R: Not in mine, Leonard.

[*Pause*]

L: Don't call me that, please.

R: Why not?

L: That's the name my mother gave me.

[*Pause*]

Just give me the glass.

R: No.

[*Pause*]

L: I'll take it, then.

R: If you take the glass . . . I'll take you.

[*Pause*]

L: How about me taking the glass without you taking me?

R: Why don't I just take you?

[*Pause*]

L: You're joking.

Joking or not, this ritual of the "social introduction" between two strangers provides a sharp and immediate contrast with Ionesco's version, without our needing to reread the text to grasp its implications. We first notice the carefully positioned pauses—six in all—that frame the dialogue. How shall we assess their purpose: to connect or to interrupt the words spoken in between? Thus, language and silence merge once again to reveal meaning, an important clue to Pinter's style and a major characteristic of what has been labeled Pinteresque in the work of his imitators.

Next we sort out the unexpected, almost riddlelike vocal turns that each character deals to the other: a game of bargaining for power, sexual or otherwise. Concrete words like "ashtray," "glass," and "carpet" call attention to the characters' most intimate props or the room's spare objects, and in the same breath they expose some unexpected message: one family member's obsession with "order and clarity"—a familiar theme in Pinter's plays. Yet another layer of meaning or possible subtext to the literal action gradually surfaces. For in speaking about his father's obsession, Lenny speaks of himself. Having moved the ashtray away from Ruth to control her desire to smoke, he asserts himself rather self-consciously by focusing on Ruth's drinking glass and in a clinical tone "relieves" her of it, whether she likes it or not. It is typical of Pinter to explore these small and intimate actions, allowing Ruth and Lenny to interrogate those social rituals others would politely take for granted. Above all, it is daring of him to reveal hidden truths through manipulated twists of language.

Then there is the sudden name-calling ritual, in which Ruth addresses Lenny as Leonard—the name his mother used to call him—and shatters his cool control. Is her reference a mere slip of the tongue that enables her to usurp a central matriarchal role? Lenny manages to regain composure by focusing once again on Ruth's glass. But this time, his earlier gentlemanly effort to "relieve" her of it becomes more driven and assaultive, as he now insists on "taking the glass" from her. But the roles have been reversed in typical Pinteresque fashion, and instead of becoming Lenny's unwilling subordinate, Ruth emerges as his consenting and triumphant adversary. It takes one short sentence, interrupted by a deeply motivated pause, to make herself quite clear to him: "If you take the glass . . . I'll take you," at which point both characters move from an objective plane of communciation to an uninhibited *psychological* center at which their souls can seek communion.

In *The Homecoming*, Pinter's themes of power, family bonding, and the reversibility of character relationships are demonstrated with a luminous candor that often teeters on the edge of the irrational but never succumbs to it. That such language tends to shock the reader has less to do with untraditional codes of behavior or with Ruth and Lenny's mutually fatal attraction, than with Pinter's daring to articulate what is customarily left unspoken. While language and silence "reveal and conceal" the subconscious desires of both characters, the dialogue's perplexing style welcomes a range of ambiguities essential to the playwright's thematic objectives. Once again, language—as a key to character and action—manifests yet another side of its purpose.

Our examples have demonstrated the different types of characters who populate the "world as a stage," as well as the varied uses of language through which they reveal themselves. In an age that thrives on verbal communication, including computer literacy and its own diverse languages, we must remain open to all modes of linguistic expression, experimental or otherwise, that will always find corresponding stage characters to voice them. Therefore, the following considerations are essential:

1. The language of the drama is best evaluated in a random and dynamic encounter of its components. Since a seasoned playgoer may attend a revival of *Medea* on one evening and a Sam Shepard play on the next, his ability to appreciate and evaluate

the language of these contrasting plays must remain flexible, objective, and critically sound—all recommended attributes of the playreader.

2. The language of the drama should be viewed on its own terms. With the realistic expectation that extensive playreading will sharpen the playreader's critical judgment, personal preferences must not disrupt our objective evaluation of one style (verse) with another (prose), or of one form (tragedy) with another (comedy), no matter where our tastes lie.

3. The language of the drama must be evaluated in relation to the characters who speak it and the actions that motivate it. Unlike other literary genres, the language of a play—as we perceive it on the printed page—never exists for its own sake or as a substitute for character and action. On the contrary, it dynamically integrates these functions.

4. The language of the drama remains a vital key to character. Just as we carefully observe the stage character for what he *does*, so must we balance our assessment of him by listening carefully to what he *says*. A phenomenon from real life is repeated on the stage, perhaps suggesting that art imitates life. (Remember Hamlet's holding "the mirror up to nature"?)

Drama and the Dimensions of Language

Our observations have shown us how the playwright's language transforms the drama into a flexible commodity. Implementing language to create characters, lay plots, and elicit themes, the drama, above all other literary genres, functions meaningfully on one of several levels: the *literal, symbolic,* and *allegorical.* Insofar as they convey some basic story line, all plays function on a literal level. On the other hand, many playwrights incorporate symbols to illuminate their characters, language, and themes, as several of our preceding examples have demonstrated. In doing so, their plays achieve symbolic repercussions. Finally, there are the exceptional examples, such as *Everyman,* in which the need for universal implication achieves the level of allegory.

Despite its economy of means and deceptively unsophisticated style, Wilder's play *Our Town* demonstrates a rare interplay of all three levels:

a search for darker purposes beyond the literal. Wilder portrays rural life in Grover's Corners, focusing on the interactions of a fictional couple, George Gibbs and Emily Webb, who grow up together, fall in love, and marry. A final outcome is Emily's death in childbirth. The playwright's unadorned, straightforward depiction of character and situation constitutes "what the story is about" and fulfills the play's literal or exact level of meaning.

Having established its primary purpose, however, we must determine whether certain characters and situations within the play are amplified by an assortment of carefully selected symbols. The crying of a newborn child, the ritual of a wedding ceremony, the solemn apparitions at a graveyard, and the white ribbon in Emily's hair as she relives her twelfth birthday would seem to convey a larger meaning that transcends their literal representations. Here the play functions on a symbolic level.

Furthermore, on a more expansive scale, it seems likely that the universality of Wilder's theme—the irrevocable cycle of birth and death—the ordinariness of characters and events, and finally, the stage setting, with its conspicuous lack of real locale and visible stage props lifts the play to the level of allegory. For most playreaders, it would seem acceptable to view Grover's Corners as a microcosm of the smaller communities that proliferate across America, just as some of the characters respectively mirror many of our own behaviors and experiences. In its soft-spoken moral and spiritual implications, *Our Town* ultimately transcends its regional dimensions to achieve the status of allegory.

Expanding the Dimensions of Drama

The playreader's specific knowledge of current events, set against even broader frameworks of history, psychology, and literature, can enrich his perception and appreciation of the drama. For example, our initial reading of Arthur Miller's *Crucible* (1953) quickly reveals a fictionalized account of the Salem witch trials of 1692. But Miller's theme of character assassination parallels a factual event in contemporary American history: the McCarthy investigation of communism in governmental affairs. Thus, the play, written more than 250 years after the Salem hysteria, is the playwright's response to an event that still remains timely in any society soiled by political turmoil. Other plays noted for their historical or sociopolitical dimensions include Maxwell

Anderson's *Winterset* (1935), which traces a young man's search for the truth and was inspired by the popular Sacco-Vanzetti case; and *Inherit the Wind* (1955), co-authored by Jerome Lawrence and Robert E. Lee. In the latter, which is based on the famous Scopes "monkey trial," the real-life figures of William Jennings Bryan and Clarence Darrow are only thinly disguised by their Brady/Drummond counterparts.

On the other hand, a playgoer's alerted responses to seemingly unrelated events can significantly enhance a drama that may no longer sustain its original impact, such as O'Neill's once-popular, now seriously dated play, *Strange Interlude* (1928). The somewhat forced, overtly melodramatic happenings of this nine-act play seem far more palatable if we consider the impact of psychology—notably the advent of Freudian analysis during the first half of the twentieth century—on its form and content. Thus, its novelistic "stream-of-consciousness" technique, which allows the highly neurotic characters to voice their private thoughts as well as their conversational dialogue, provides continual fascination once we have grasped its underlying premise. Contrasted with O'Neill's later and far superior *Long Day's Journey into Night,* the playreader walks away with a considerably richer impression of O'Neill's versatility and growth as a dramatist.

Drama versus Docudrama

In none of these plays, however, have the playwrights attempted to document factual data, transforming their playscripts into historical or sociological tracts. This is not their responsibility, despite the powerful impact of Euripides's earliest antiwar play, *The Trojan Women,* or Shakespeare's historicopolitical tragedy, *Julius Caesar.* We know how classics speak to us through their timely characters, powerful language, and gripping plots. Yet a brief backward glance will attest to modern drama's penchant for realism and naturalism and, in particular, its more recent preoccupation with documentary-like enactments of popular, often controversial themes. If we come to the playscript without prior knowledge of the protagonist's rare disease, Bernard Pomerance's Brechtian chronicle of John Merrick's life in *The Elephant Man* (1979) will provide us with the tragic details. If the consequences of America's involvement in Vietnam have been slow to capture the imaginations of playwrights, despite Rabe's chilling *Pavlo Hummel* and *Sticks and Bones* (1972), Emily Mann's *Still Life* (1980) reminds us that its tragic effects privately haunt its victims and their families. As the impact of AIDS surfaced into a worldwide phenomenon, William Hoffman's *As Is* (1985) and Larry Kramer's *Normal Heart* (1985) do not miss the opportunity to inform us of its social and political ramifications. With cold, documentary-like precision, these scripts have exposed us to the darker side of our lives.

How to Evaluate the Playscript

As we prepare to discuss or write about a particular play, the following topical framework should facilitate our analysis. Using one of O'Neill's late plays, the model focuses on the range of seven categories for possible investigation:

[1] Offer an Introductory Assessment

The title *Long Day's Journey into Night* accurately suggests to us the unified time span—about sixteen hours—during which the telescoped and consecutive actions of the play's four acts transpire. The realistic setting, which exemplifies the slice-of-life technique, is the "living room of James Tyrone's summer house on a morning in August, 1912." The cast of characters—a father, James Tyrone; his wife, Mary; an elder son, Jamie; and a younger one, Edmund—alerts us that O'Neill's plot will explore family relationships. We suspect that the presence of a fifth character, a servant named Cathleen, comments ironically on the family's self-sufficiency and social status. O'Neill's handling of time, setting, and dramatic action, carefully balanced by a network of closely knit characters, produces an economy of style that is contemporary in tone and classical in design.

[2] Evaluate the Physical Setting

In his description of the set, O'Neill draws our attention to a detailed list of authors, whose works—all literary, philosophical, sociological, and historical—fill the two bookcases of the parlor walls and reveal the background, interests, and psychological makeup of the Tyrones. As the action of the play gradually unfolds, we discover that the countless quotations or literary allusions spouted by the characters are purposely drawn from the works of these authors. The other significant set detail is that at stage center is "a round table with a green shaded reading lamp, the cord plugged in one of the four sockets in the chandelier above. Around the table within reading-light range are four chairs." The notable use of the living room as the singular arena for interaction lures us, as well as its inhabitants, to a focal area and asserts that the play will be *character-centered*. Above all, the physical environment is matched by an emotional one, conducive to outspoken, confessional character confrontations.

[3]   Pay Close Attention to What the Character Descriptions Tell Us

It is wise to note that the first character description we receive belongs to Mary Tyrone, also the only female of this family. At fifty-four, her graceful figure, now grown plump "is distinctly Irish in type." What impresses us, however, is "her extreme nervousness. Her hands are never still. They were once beautiful hands . . . but rheumatism has knotted the joints and warped the fingers." Her husband, James, once a famous actor, allows his profession to show "in all his unconscious habits of speech, movement and gesture." He wears "a threadbare, ready-made, grey sack suit and shineless black shoes." At thirty-three, Jamie, the elder son, is still good-looking, despite his "signs of premature disintegration" and "marks of dissipation." Edmund, the last to be described, is ten years younger than his brother, with a nervousness that is "noticeably like his mother's." His eyes "appear feverish and his cheeks are sunken." His skin "has a parched sallowness." On the basis of O'Neill's hierarchy of character introductions and descriptions, we detect the curious bond established between Mary Tyrone and her younger son, and, more important, all four characters are marked by certain identifiable weaknesses.

[4]   Provide a Succinct Analysis of the Plot

By the conclusion of the first act, character dialogue and behaviors have begun to mirror O'Neill's initial descriptions of the four Tyrones, revealing truths that will embellish the plot and culminate in an assortment of smaller themes: Jamie is an alcoholic whose dissipation seems incorrigible; Edmund's lingering "summer cold" points to tuberculosis; Tyrone's stinginess underscores the lack of proper medical treatment given to his younger son; and, finally, Mary Tyrone's

"nervousness" is the result of her addiction to morphine, first admin-
istered to her by a quack doctor during Edmund's difficult birth
twenty-three years earlier. While both sons are concerned about their
mother's behavior, and Tyrone grows increasingly attentive to her
needs, O'Neill's balanced, three-dimensional depictions of these characters contribute to a disturbing family portrait.

Throughout the second act, O'Neill further exposes the relationships
of the Tyrone family by investigating its past. This is heightened by the
effects of alcohol and morphine, which allow each character to confess
a side of his nature that transcends the literal present time of the
action. O'Neill's dramatic achievement is considerable: within a
unified time, place, and action, we examine the lives of the Tyrones in
microscopic detail, as their journey is transformed into a symbolic "dark
night of the soul."

The climactic third act allows Mary Tyrone to pour out her sorrows
to the servant girl, Cathleen, who, among her practical functions in
the play, has become Mary's confidante. O'Neill's altered description of
Mary, as "paler than before" with eyes that "shine with unnatural
brilliance," assures us that her addiction is insidious and real. We
confront two significant details in this act, both of which constitute the
play's climax: that Edmund's summer cold is, indeed, tubercular and
will require his entering a sanatorium; and that Mary's morphine
addiction is openly acknowledged by her husband and sons. Despite
these parallel disclosures, which remain curiously linked through the
mother/son relationship established earlier, Mary Tyrone emerges as
the central protagonist in a conflict that incorporates four protagonists
struggling against time and fate.

The denouement of O'Neill's exploration lasts the duration of the
play's fourth act: we suspect a bonding between father and sons, as well
as between brothers, will strengthen their mutual love and understanding and enable them to confront Mary Tyrone in her tragic disintegration and return to the past, when she first "fell in love with James
Tyrone and was so happy for a time."

[5] Highlight the Play's Most Significant Production Ingredient

Three well-timed sound effects contribute to the action and theme of
the play and constitute its major production ingredient. The first two
occur simultaneously in the third and fourth acts, which unfold at

six-thirty in the evening and around midnight, respectively. The sound of a foghorn is "heard at regular intervals, moaning like a mournful whale in labor, and from the harbor itself, intermittently, comes the warning ringing of bells on yachts at anchor." Both noises (sound effects) herald the approach of fog and symbolically parallel the increased intake of alcohol (Tyrone and sons) and morphine (Mary). At the peak of their abuses and in the midst of explicit vocal candor, Edmund appropriately concludes that "stammering is the native eloquence of us fog people."

Then, quite suddenly, "someone starts playing the piano [in the front parlor]—the opening of one of Chopin's simpler waltzes, done with a forgetful, stiff-fingered groping, as if an awkward schoolgirl were practicing it for the first time." This musical effect finalizes Mary's total submission to morphine, her return to the past, to a girlhood that represents the only happiness she has ever known.

[6] Observe the Play's Language; Summarize Its Theme

O'Neill's language is realistic and poetic, as it mixes images, symbols, and literary allusion with coarse, confrontational speech. The play's principal theme, so intricately interwoven with Mary Tyrone's merging of past with present, is spoken by her: "The past is the present, isn't it? It's the future, too. We all try to lie out of that but life won't let us." The implied *unalterability of one's fate,* a universal theme voiced earlier in Greek drama, suits O'Neill's vision as well. While emphasizing the play's literal level of meaning, it also recalls key symbols of real and psychological time and strives toward some universal, if not wholly allegorical, view.

[7] Cite a Significant Issue Raised by the Play

The play, which stands strongly on its own dramaturgical merits, also prompts our judging it from a more heightened perspective: in short, a case for drama versus biography. As it is an autobiographical work, we must further consider our responsibility to consider its real and fictional parallels *after* the fact of the play itself. The play exposes O'Neill's own family, in much the same way that the undisguised "Tyrones" provide the playwright with viable stage characters and a valid subject. Although the attraction seems mutual, these personal facts, which exist outside the play, must not blur our objective literary evaluation. Autobiographical data neither determine the playwright's skills nor enhance the play's effectiveness. Nevertheless, the availability of such information, although it must not take precedence over the play itself, can ultimately enrich our understanding of the playwright's art.

Themes for Analysis: Language

The properties of language inspire many exciting themes, all of which must be supported by careful and specific references to the text. Our consideration of topical statements reflects a range of concerns for the use of language and its numerous components. Is there a *language of tragedy* with properties that distinguish it from a *language of comedy*? In the light of our preceding discussion, the following statements would suggest that there is: [In each of the first three categories, selected topics designated by the asterisk (*) have been annotated with short questions for additional clarification.]

1. "What the Soul-Searching Soliloquies and Dialogues of Sophocles's *Oedipus Rex* Tell Us."

*2. "The Confessional Language of Brutus Jones's Soliloquy in O'Neill's *Emperor Jones*." (Exactly how does O'Neill use the nonrealistic convention of soliloquy to advance character development and action in his play? Does he succeed?)

3. "The Havoc of Misinterpreted Messages in Shakespeare's *King Lear*."

*4. "The Illogical Logic of Ionesco's *Bald Soprano*." (How does the playwright use language to support the premises of absurdity in this play? Does he ignore the playreader's capacity to reason or "make sense" of his language altogether? Or does his use of language reflect a subtle design?)

5. "Intellectual Comedy and Words of Love in Stoppard's *Real Thing*."

*6. "Comical Twists-of-the-Tongue in the 'Pyramus and Thisbe' Sequence of Shakespeare's *Midsummer Night's Dream.*" (How does Shakespeare's comical language reflect the idiosyncrasies of each of the mechanicals? Does it gain a special resonance in the mouths of such characters?)

Suggesting that there may be more to the character's message than at first reaches our ears, the following statements point to the role of *language as subtext* in the drama:

*1. "The Straight-Talking Double-Talk of Mamet's *Glengarry Glen Ross.*" (Is there a reality underlying the quickly paced double-talking style of this play? What does it reveal about the characters and their ethics? Does Mamet's purpose succeed as a *playreading* experience?)

*2. "Words as Weapons in Shepard's *Tooth of Crime.*" (Can we itemize the unusual vocabulary—both word choices and images—uttered by Shepard's characters and show how they foreshadow or support the physical showdown that serves as climax to the play?)

3. "Words of Menace in Pinter's *Homecoming.*"

4. "Decoding Messages in Shepard's *Buried Child.*"

*5. "What Beckett's *Waiting for Godot* Is Really About." (How does language contribute to the mystery and fascination of Beckett's characters and theme? Does the play's language point to any valid and tangible conclusions?)

6. "What Happened at the Zoo in Albee's *Zoo Story?*"

It is essential that we evaluate the effects of *imagery* and *symbolism*, both subtle and explicit, in the drama:

1. "Images of Disease in Shakespeare's *Hamlet.*"

*2. "The Subconscious Equine Imagery of Shaffer's *Equus.*" (Does the verbal imagery reflect an attention-getting, purely theatrical purpose, or does it serve a legitimate dramatic end?)

   3. "Domestic Images in the World of Wilder's *Our Town*."

*4. "Evaluating Laura's Imaginary World in Williams's *Glass Menagerie*." (How do the play's production ingredients contribute to Williams's purpose? Is his reputation as symbolist enhanced by this play?)

   5. "Symbolic Clues to Meaning in Ibsen's *Hedda Gabler*."

*6. "What the Cherry Orchard Represents in Chekhov's *Cherry Orchard*." (How are the realistic events of Chekhov's play enhanced by overtly symbolic allusions to the cherry orchard? Are both realistic and symbolic levels mutually compatible?)

Undoubtedly the most powerful property of language is its expression of theme, the central point or underlying idea of the play. Once we have uncovered these underlying ideas, we must shape our findings into concise, accessible statements. The following sets of alternatives suggest a variety of workable themes, all derived from the central point of each play in question:

Marsha Norman, *'night, mother*:
   "Fatal Choices in . . ."
   "Love and the Meaning of Life in . . ."

Samuel Beckett, *Waiting for Godot*:
   "The Absurdity of Existence in . . ."
   "Living with Hope in . . ."

Henrik Ibsen, *A Doll's House*:
   "Sexual Equality in . . ."
   "Selfhood and Marriage in . . ."

William Shakespeare, *Hamlet*:
   "Private Revenge versus Public Justice in . . ."
   "The Cosmic Setting of Human Life in . . ."

William Congreve, *The Way of the World*:
   "The Inconstancy of Love in . . ."
   "Formulas for Marriage in . . ."

Lorraine Hansberry, *A Raisin in the Sun:*
  "Dreams Deferred in . . ."
  "Human Dignity in . . ."

Sam Shepard, *The Tooth of Crime:*
  "Survival as Ritual in . . ."
  "The Incurable Violence of the American Psyche
  in . . ."

Edward Albee, *The Zoo Story:*
  "Human Isolation in . . ."
  "An Outcast's Struggle to Belong in . . ."

Jean-Claude van Itallie, *The Serpent:*
  "Remaking the Past in . . ."
  "Searching for Ourselves in . . ."

David Rabe, *The Basic Training of Pavlo Hummel:*
  "Growing up to Die in . . ."
  "Selfhood and Discovery in . . ."

Elmer Rice, *The Adding Machine:*
  "The Everyman Story as Retold in . . ."
  "The Dehumanized World of . . ."

Our final consideration of language responds to its dimensions or levels of meaning, reminding us of how the repercussions of a play can extend beyond its literal setting and incidents. The following themes investigate these dimensions:

*1. "Restaging the Events of History in Lawrence and Lee's *Inherit the Wind.*" (Our discussion should not only consider the ways in which the play "theatricalizes" the principle characters and events of the famous Monkey Trial but should also evaluate the conflict, waged through language, between its two central protagonists.)

*2. "Drama versus Docudrama in Kramer's *Normal Heart.* (Focusing on the playwright's use of verbal propaganda, our discussion should analyze the impact of the AIDS phenomenon on the network of characters set before us.)

*3. "Interpreting Allegorical Parallels in Wilder's *Skin of Our Teeth.*" (While our discussion should consider the assortment of symbolic characters and events surrounding the Everyman protagonist and his family, it is Wilder's language that ultimately transforms the play into comic allegory.)

*4. "How a Freudian Interpretation Can Alter Our View of O'Neill's *Desire under the Elms.*" (Our discussion should show how O'Neill's language defines the psychological motivations of his characters and elevates their predicament to the level of tragedy.)

*5. "The War at Home in Mann's *Still Life.*" (Our discussion should evaluate the playwright's use of the "personal interview"— offstage and on—to document and authenticate the dialogue of her stage characters.)

CHAPTER SEVEN
APPROACHING THE MISE-EN-SCÈNE

Be cheerful, sir.
Our revels now are ended.
—*The Tempest*, IV, i

We might construe Shakespeare's optimism to imply that the "revels" of imagining the components of any play will eventually induce some final, cohesive, theatrical whole. From the start of our investigation, we have occasionally doubled as play director in itemizing our many responsibilities toward the recreation of the play: understanding its dramatic structure, identifying its principal and supporting characters, envisioning its stage environment through detailed scenic descriptions, sound, and costumes effects. Once we have sorted out these elements, however, our most challenging task—much like the play director's—involves the *artistic arrangement of these components, as they emerge in our playreading imagination, into an integrated stage picture,* a process that constitutes and defines the *mise-en-scène.*

Whether we simply peruse the script or analyze it carefully for meaning and impact, we eventually grasp its design: a unified shape or a visual impression of its transformation from the printed page. Yet there is no single approach to *mise-en-scène,* just as the actualized stage production of one director will often contrast radically with another's. Similar directorial choices confront our mind's eye as it conjures an effective stage composition. To achieve this, we must:

1. *Visualize* the play in relation to the conventions of the theatre for which it was written (e.g., classical Greek, Elizabethan, contemporary).

2. *Select* the play's most striking or notable feature, whether related to plot, character, or scenic description, as a starting point in your imagination.

3. *Develop* a closer playreader/character relationship, by identifying on some level with one of the play's characters.

4. *Determine* the size and shape of the imaginary performance space in order to expand your view—and viewpoint—of the play.

Not all of the above considerations will surface in a single playreading or converge in any one play. But the information gathered from them should provide helpful background for an *imaginary* reconstruction. The process is gradual and dynamic, demanding that we investigate the literary text for as long as it nurtures and provokes our response. Relating to a play most recently discussed, for example, let us assume we have established a workable *mise-en-scène* for *Long Day's Journey into Night* through an earlier first reading of the play. A return to the text, whether a week or a year later, should embellish our initial impressions. Our earlier recollection of the four Tyrones, once barely delineated in their indifferently furnished drawing room, can be replaced by a more effective arrangement: we now visualize a nervously animated Mary Tyrone in contrast to the ominous, more stationary figures of husband and sons, while silent fog and noisy foghorns embellish our imaginations to establish their drug-induced isolation. Our visualization of this latter *mise-en-scène* accommodates the discoveries of a more sensitive and alert playreader. It also demonstrates how our former consideration of those less evident textual clues prevented our appreciating fully the play's format, character strategies, and scenic shadings, all of which needed more time to avail themselves to us. The following approaches explore some of these alternatives.

Approaching Classical Design

Although *The Trojan Women* is virtually plotless and almost entirely without action—a feature that distinguishes it from its classical counterparts—several factors influence our approach to its *mise-en-scène:* the small cast with its intimate character encounters, its adherence to the unities, and its moral purpose. Since her focal position engages Hecuba in a series of confrontations with a mad daughter, Cassandra; a widowed daughter-in-law, Andromache; an angry Menelaus; and a blameworthy Helen, we undoubtedly recognize the bereft queen as the play's most notable presence. We gradually perceive the arrangement of lengthy monologues, interrupted by short verbal character interactions, to be *circular* in design and facilitated further through a conventional adherence to the unities of time, place and action.

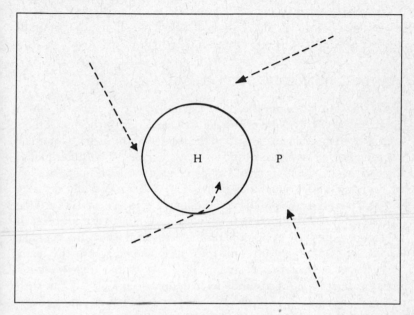

Visual pattern: circular; playreader (P) at periphery.

To establish a closer relationship between playreader and stage character, essential for Euripides's intimate network of characters and limited stage action, we might envision a circular playing area in the conventional Greek style but significantly reduced to an arena space. Next we dissolve the safe "aesthetic distance" by establishing our *imaginary perspective* from any point of the circular periphery and daring to come so emotionally close to Hecuba as to imagine her tears. Since Hecuba initiates and closes the static action, it is essential that we consistently highlight her in our mind's eye as the personified force of the playwright's antiwar message. To achieve this, we may "block" her at stage center, in a nearly collapsed physical state, as each of her antagonists enters the performance space and encircles her slowly while unleashing his woe. To reinforce the play's universality in our projection of this gripping *mise-en-scène*, we are free to imagine a burning red sky as the single perpetual backdrop to these stark dialogues on the horrors of war, or to juxtapose the characters' conventional "tragic masks" with the faces of the contemporary female victims of Hiroshima or My Lai. Just as the play director often contemporizes the *mise-en-scène* to incorporate the modern sensibility of his spectator, so must we introduce whatever timely ingredient will strengthen our grasp of the words before us.

Approaching Elizabethan Design

Two factors determine the more expansive *mise-en-scène* of Shakespeare's *Midsummer Night's Dream:* the variety of intricate subplots stemming from an abandonment of the unities, and the sharp interplay between the real and green (fairy) worlds. In contrast with Euripides's circular design, the more than two dozen characters who populate our imagination serve a humorous rather than didactic end and devise a different set of conventions to accomplish this. The most striking feature is the play's multiple actions, which, seeming to intrude on each other, are rounded to completion in the play's final scene: the marriage of Theseus and Hippolyta. This royal pair, around whom the many characters and situations revolve, incorporates us into their event—a unifying device that opens and closes the play—and provides us with some objective point of view. We are left with several alternatives, however, all provided by the flexible conventions Shakespeare has carefully established and some of which emerge as helpful clues to the romantic confusion at hand.

The first clue is found in Shakespeare's language. Since the multiple subplots originally unfolded in the Elizabethan daylight, with minimal sets or props, stage directions were automatically incorporated into character dialogue and pointed to the half-dozen locales contained within the play. The first approach to a workable *mise-en-scène* encourages us to imagine each of the subplots unfolding in the same physical space, one followed by the other. This is facilitated through Shakespeare's built-in scenic descriptions, which assist our imaginations in processing the rapid succession of stage happenings. A more striking alternative, however, is the designation of two separate physical spaces to incorporate the dynamic *interplay* of real and green world characters. If we envision a deep thrust apron to accommodate the actions of the real-world characters and an elevated upstage level to accommodate the green world, the intrusion of one world upon the other will be more effortlessly integrated. Once these separate kingdoms of colorful characters are carefully set into motion, provided we have established our *imaginary perspective* at the base of the thrust, our *mise-en-scène* will enhance the play's major thematic purpose: the integrative powers of love.

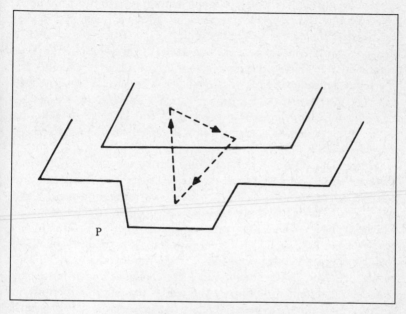

Visual pattern: interplay; playreader (P) at thrust.

Approaching Modern Design

Despite its fairly linear arrangement, an approach to the *mise-en-scène* of Luigi Pirandello's *Six Characters in Search of an Author* (1921) is more complex, as its premise and theme—the often unsteady and dangerous balance between illusion and reality—challenge the nature of real versus stage life. Before a workable *mise-en-scène* can be established, however, a brief description of the play's premise seems in order: as a group of professional actors rehearses a play, a family of six characters suddenly appears in their midst from nowhere, claiming they are figures from a real-life drama, now abandoned by their playwright.

To the dissatisfaction of his professional company, the Manager is persuaded to let these strangers enact their scenes, and then another interruption surfaces: which group of players is more prepared to portray the truth? The six characters who have actually *lived* it or the professional players who have been trained to *enact* it?

A brief but vital stage description that accompanies the intrusive appearance of the six characters is our sharpest clue to the atmosphere and tension of the play: "A tenuous light surrounds them, almost as if irradiated by them—the faint breath of their fantastic reality." Unlike the green-world characters of *A Midsummer Night's Dream*, who exist independently of the other characters in the play, Pirandello's six characters refuse to be dismissed so easily or to be relegated to enacting their tragic scenes in a separate corner of the stage. We cannot ignore their insistence on sharing the same space with the actors of the company and on being accepted for their individual, palpable realities.

We are challenged in a very different way by the play-within-a-play strategy Pirandello has given us. As this is a striking characteristic and possible key to an effective *mise-en-scène*, we recognize that the two dozen or so "actors of the company" are no more than extraneous supporting figures of an intimate dramatic landscape. In constructing its *mise-en-scène*, we should balance the "fantastic reality" of these characters against the choruslike antagonism of the players who outnumber them. If our imaginations are challenged even further by Pirandello's attempt to juxtapose the worlds of reality and fantasy in order to emphasize their essential relativity, however, an *environmental* approach would complement the playwright's purpose and would enhance our appreciation of the play's unique "theatricality." The concept of environmental theatre, as we have seen elsewhere, allows both the performer and the spectator *to inhabit the same space*. Let us imagine that the "actors of the company" are preparing their play in a spacious rehearsal hall instead of the conventional picture frame set, and let us perceive ourselves as unseen spectators who sit among them. Suddenly the six characters enter and "stop by the door at back of stage," before approaching the area where the actors are presently rehearsing their own play. This flexible, scrambled arrangement of spectator and actor placements intensifies the interchangeable relationships among the professional actors, the six characters, and ourselves. Thus, we imagine ourselves at the psychological center of the antagonism between both sets of players. This arrangement not only strengthens Pirandello's play-within-a-play strategy but also incorporates us into the play's theme: that man cannot live without illusion.

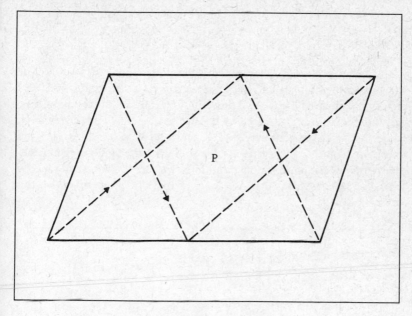

Visual pattern: Environmental; play-reader (P) at center.

Approaching Contemporary Design

Sam Shepard's *Tooth of Crime*, a "Play with Music in Two Acts," projects a very different *mise-en-scène*, primarily dictated by its one-to-one character struggle and *confrontational* Brechtian musical interludes, all purposely designed to provoke our "spectator" responses. This intimate rock-and-roll Western, set in a futuristic present, requires the atmosphere of a "bare stage." Shepard's additional request that "the band should be hidden" further underscores the work as a drama facilitated by music. The hard rock statement sung by the protagonist Hoss, who is dressed "in black rocker gear with silver studs and black kid gloves," sets up several dramatic and musical expectations:

So here's another illusion to add to your confusion
Of the way things are
Everybody's doin' time for somebody else's crime and

I can't swim for the waves in the ocean
All the heroes is dyin' like flies they say it's a sign a' the times
And everybody's walkin' asleep eyes open—eyes open

The lyrics of the song exclaim Hoss's preoccupation with survival and suggest a *mise-en-scène* that will remain flexible to the conflicting personal and professional halves of his life. Perceiving him at such close range, we might imagine the stage action as a dissection of Hoss's emotional anatomy and visualize him on an elevated boxing-ring platform not unlike those used by popular rock artists. Perhaps the rock band sits under the platform, shielded by a gauzy veil that exposes the musicians slightly when certain lights spill from the performance space. Furthermore, our imagination should incorporate the band as a raucous character whose pulsating, noisy contribution competes with the dramatic action.

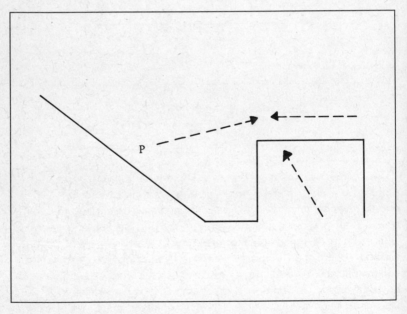

Visual pattern: confrontation; play-reader (P) at counterpoint.

Can we imagine ourselves perched on sharply raked bleachers that compel us to face Hoss at eye level? *The Tooth of Crime* is about confrontation of the cruelest sort: its deceptively cool premise—Hoss's fight to stay at the top of the musical charts—is ultimately about the erosion of fame and our own struggle-to-the-death attempts to survive. That is, until Crow enters the scene, with a lyric that sells us his own brand of sadistic assurance:

> I coulda' gone the route—of beggin' for my life
> Crawlin' on my hands and knees
> But there ain't no Gods or saviors who'll give you
>   flesh and blood
> Its time to squeeze the trigger
> But I believe in my mask—The man I made up is me
> And I believe in my dance—And my destiny

And squeeze the trigger he does! But not before a series of operatic musical rounds, structured like combat in a boxing arena, is stridently played out for us:

> Hoss and Crow begin to move to the music, not really dancing but feeling the power in their movements through the music. They each pick up microphones. They begin their assaults just talking the words in rhythmic patterns, sometimes going with the music, sometimes counterpointing it. As the round progresses the music builds with drums and piano coming in, maybe a rhythm guitar too. Their voices build so that sometimes they sing the words or shout. The words remain as intelligible as possible like a sort of talking opera.

Our imagination integrates both the musical and dramatic iconography that fashions this lively *mise-en-scène* and embellishes Shepard's surreal, almost kaleidoscopic vision. Suspecting that the playwright will allow but one winner, we perceive these rock-artist pugilists as colorful cartoon characters who play at destruction only to discover that their ritual is for keeps.

Playreading and the Musical Format

Our approach to establishing a *mise-en-scène* for Shepard's *Tooth of Crime*, a play in which the vital element of music remains *subordinate* to the dramatic action, prompts our concern for a theatrical format in which the contribution of music is *primary*. Although our horizontal perspective has already shown us that drama is synonymous with music and dance *outside* the Western tradition, the American "musical" is a legitimate form that combines drama, music, and dance, and it enjoys great popularity with contemporary playgoers. While its fairly unsophisticated structure has evolved into a more complex one in recent decades, the text or "book" for any musical is always available for our reading pleasure, despite the absence of music and choreography (dance). With our mind's eye more adept at reconstructing these elements from the printed page into a meaningful theatrical experience, we can effectively envision some of the more spectacular effects that highlight this indigenous American tradition.

Not coincidentally, our list of conventional performance components—plot, character, including the prominently featured "chorus," and spectacle—characterizes a range of styles from classical drama to the American musical. As perceptive playreaders, we anticipate smooth transitions from one style to another, especially if our tastes are sufficiently flexible to incorporate the radically altered treatment of these components. To begin with, the popular musical has never competed with serious drama, even when it has borrowed from its sources. And while the entertainment value of the musical has often preceded its reputation, its dramatic impact has frequently proved comparable to "legitimate" drama. On the other hand, the musical format requires the collaborative efforts and collective imagination of numerous contributors such as musical composer, lyricist, director, choreographer, set and costume designers to fashion a larger-than-life performance piece in which the concern for realism is often intentionally underplayed. Finally, we need to be more generous, or at least expansive, with our own playreading imagination to accommodate the musical's heightened arrangement of these multiple visual and aural components.

We should approach the text of the musical knowing that:

1. The plot is often adapted from an established literary source: For example, the Richard Rodgers and Oscar Hammerstein musical *Carousel* (1945) is based on Ferenc Molnar's play *Liliom* (1909). Selected scenes and characters from the Roman comedies of Terence and Plautus are the sources of Sondheim and Gelbart's *A Funny Thing Happened on the Way to the Forum*. The Roger

Miller and William Hauptmann musical, *Big River* (1984), is inspired by Mark Twain's novel *The Adventures of Huckleberry Finn.* Unless the book is original—that is, totally independent of an outside source—our appreciation of the musical version will be considerably enhanced by an acquaintance with the work on which it is based.

2. Both plot and characters are—or should be—expanded through the dimensions of music and choreography: For example, while contemplating his future as the father of a yet unborn child in the song "Soliloquy" from *Carousel,* Billy Bigelow's humor, irony, and introspection reveal a psychological makeup and depth of character that heighten our responses toward him. In Lerner and Loewe's *My Fair Lady* (1955), Eliza Doolittle's elocution exercise is wittily expressed to the tangolike rhythms of "The Rain in Spain," a song that also points to her transformation from flower girl to duchess. In the Bernstein-Laurents-Sondheim musical, *West Side Story* (1957), inspired by Shakespeare's tragedy *Romeo and Juliet,* the music and choreography of "The Dance at the Gym" foreshadow the gang rumble that precipitates the musical's stirring climax.

3. The musical traditionally unfolds in less intimate performance spaces to accommodate its elaborate physical sets, large casts, and choruses. Despite these grand-scale production ingredients, however, the plot is often drawn along far simpler lines, providing contrast with its more embellished musical sequences.

4. Since the mid-1970s, musicals have grown more "operatic" in style, so audiences have come to expect storytelling through continuous music. In such performances, singing no longer contrasts with spoken dialogue; it virtually sustains the drama. Andrew Lloyd Webber and Tim Rice's *Jesus Christ Superstar* (1970) and *Evita* (1978) are popular forerunners of this style. The Schonberg-Boubil-Kretzmer musical *Les Miserables* (1985), based on the Victor Hugo novel, and Webber's *Phantom of the Opera* (1987) have innovated the format by implementing highly mechanized stage machinery, thus challenging our visualization of *mise-en-scène.*

Highlighting the Dimensions of the American Musical

Like any reputable literary drama, the American musical demon-strates a variety of styles that, once recognized by the playreader, will enhance his appreciation of this form. The range and flexibility of the popular musical is demonstrated by the following five examples:

1. *Kiss Me Kate* (1948) boasts the bouncy music and clever lyrics of Cole Porter and a witty "gangster" script by Sam and Bella Spewack. But its greatest inspiration belongs to Shakespeare, whose quarreling lovers, Katharine and Petruchio, surface once more to provide the sparks in this comedy-within-a-musical-comedy. Their infamous seduction, which we have discussed earlier, becomes a show-stopper for the two real-life actors—and quarreling lovers—touring in a production of *The Taming of the Shrew*. While there is neither depth nor credibility to the musical's plot, its two eccentric and contrasting protago-nists, surrounded by a chorus of caricatures, compel our attention through their amiably underhanded maneuvers and smartly Shakespearean paraphrases. Lili's (i.e., Kate's) hilarious "I Hate Men" renounces the opposite sex, while Fred's (i.e., Petruchio's) persuasive lyric, "So in Love with You Am I," takes a hint or two from Shakespeare and ultimately wins Lili over. With its unabashed emphasis on character over plot, *Kiss Me Kate* sets a standard for the musical-comedy format that will be often imitated but rarely matched.

2. *Fiddler on the Roof* (1964) loses none of the Sholom Aleichem magic in this Jerry Bock–Sheldon Harnick musicalization of the famous Tevye stories. In fact, this poignant drama of Jewish life in revolutionary Russia at the turn of the century is considerably enhanced by its lyricized themes of fortitude, humor, and courage in the midst of political adversity and oppression. As playreaders, we are enchanted by the charismatic protagonist, Tevye, who unifies the characters and actions of this musical drama. Lyrics to such songs as "Tradition" (the strengths of family and commu-nity), "If I Were a Rich Man" (Tevye's dream of the good life), and "Sunrise, Sunset" (life's fulfillment through love) illuminate the story line and preserve the philosophical musings of the Aleichem original. Finally, we respond to *Fiddler's* universality,

which is powerfully captured through character, plot, and language.

3. *Man of La Mancha* (1965) is a musical tribute to the enduring, eponymous Don Quixote. Dale Wasserman's book is suggested by the life and works of Miguel de Cervantes. It has music by Mitch Leigh and lyrics by Joe Darion. Set against a stark, abstractly constructed landscape, the effective blend of historical and fictional characters and events is led by two aged and weary *braggart soldiers*—Quixote and Sancho—whose adventures once again challenge the fabric of our theatrical imagination. Enlivened by the elements of melodrama and romance (including a rape scene and the Spanish Inquisition), this long one-act musical urges us to live life to its fullest, a message eloquently expressed in Quixote's climactic "quest" to dream "the impossible dream." Such rich character portraits and gripping theme finally distinguish this musical from its conventional counterparts.

4. *1776* (1969) remains notable for its strikingly original concept: a musical surrounding the signing of the Declaration of Independence. With a book by Peter Stone and music and lyrics by Sherman Edwards, its sharply etched and integrated scenes— seven in all—provide a moment-to-moment countdown to the historical event itself. The final stage picture freezes to suggest the familiar Trumbull painting of the famous co-signers. On his journey toward the musical's stirring finale, however, the playreader encounters a collection of imaginatively detailed character portraits, highlighted by some gossipy and domesticated glimpses of John Adams, Ben Franklin, and Thomas Jefferson. Jefferson's wife Martha tells us that he communicates with his family through music ("He Plays the Violin!"). The overall theatricalized concept, which makes no attempt to offer us a factual reconstruction, presents exuberant themes of human freedom versus slavery ("Molasses to Rum"), individualism, and in the lyric titled "Is Anybody There?," brotherly love.

5. *A Chorus Line* (1975), as conceived by Michael Bennett, evokes the emotional landscape Sam Shepard gave us in *The Tooth of Crime*. However, Bennett's *struggle-to-survive* metaphor is transformed into a high-kicking chorus line, where the talented

contestants are a dime-a-dozen and dispensable. The powerful book by James Kirkwood and Nicholas Dante, who also participated in the lengthy, collective rehearsal process under which much of the play's improvisatory dialogue surfaced, is enhanced by Marvin Hamlisch's driving musical rhythms and Edward Kleban's penetrating lyrics. Furthermore, in retrieving the unconventional monologue format, the story allows its characters to reveal their souls through speech and song, until all of the confessions coalesce into a contemporary allegory in which each of us is represented. Bennett forces his characters to hold up their masks—in the form of head shots—while the set's backdrop of gigantic mirrors continually reflects the audience. His premise proves workable, for the playreader has little difficulty coming to terms with these characters' outspokenness: those who find their dance vocations "At the Ballet"; the adolescent basketball player who loses his youth and innocence—all at the same time—in "Hello Twelve, Hello Thirteen, Hello Love"; or the chorus's optimism as it anticipates "tomorrow" in the haunting lyric "What I Did for Love." A *Chorus Line*'s balance of forthright characters, uninhibited dramatic action, and universal theme of the "survival of the fittest" reinforces the versatility and natural appeal of the American musical tradition.

The Novel as Musical Drama

Big River, described as "a musical play," recreates many of the characters and events of Twain's adventure novel, all of which are framed against the Mississippi River Valley sometime in the late 1840s. In the published text for the musical, the scene is set simply, sharply, and most imaginatively:

> The backdrop is a sepia-toned etching of the Mississippi River, flowing toward us from the horizon. The river spills out of the backdrop, becoming a flight of wooden steps which descend to the stage floor. There, it flows as wooden planking on down to the apron. At the opening of the play, this is concealed by a scrim which looks like a gilded oval picture frame. Some elements are flown; some scenes are played on platforms, resembling

piers, that track out of the wings. The raft, also tracked, can rotate and travel across the stage simultaneously.

Mindful of the central importance of the Mississippi River, in both its symbolic and practical functions, the set designer, Heidi Landesman, does more than provide an environment for this "action" musical; she helps our mind's eye to encompass the "look and feel" of stagecraft popular at the time in which Twain's story is set. The gilded oval picture frame, which is "flown"—that is, *mechanically introduced into the stage set*, then quickly removed—lends attractive storytelling touches to the proceedings. Suddenly the silent figure of Mr. Twain appears before it, followed by Huck Finn who, as the musical's narrator-protagonist, introduces himself and his friend, a runaway slave named Jim. Once the oval frontispiece is flown out, we are in the home of the Widow Douglas, with furniture pieces wheeled in on "tracks" from both "wings" (sides of the stage). We are immediately incorporated into the first of Huck's domestic predicaments, before he seeks refuge on the "big river."

Handling the Libretto

Once we have settled into the story of the play, our encounter with the libretto (song lyrics) should be incorporated, despite the lack of musical accompaniment. In *Big River* more than seventeen musical "numbers" jump off the page like rhythmic patter to animate the characters and actions of the play. The libretto calls for some responsible "sounding out," of course, as the integration of prose and lyrical formatting considerably alters the external appearance and internal pace of the conventional playscript. Thematically consistent with Twain's novel, as well as with the spoken dialogue of the musical's book, the libretto reflects themes of friendship, flight, freedom, and survival. A passage of dialogue predictably builds to a point where the insertion of a song embellishes the scene's effectiveness and provides a certain lift of intensity essential to its familiar rising and falling actions.

In the tradition of most successful musicals, the libretto for *Big River* defines character, advances stage action, and echoes themes. Just seconds into the musical, the Widow Douglas and her sister, Miss Watson, offer Huck the kind of advice he certainly has no intention of following. In "Do Ya Wanna Go to Heaven," they alternately sing out:

Loókă hére, Húck, dŏ yŏu wánnă gó tŏ héavĕn
Dŏ yŏu wánnă gó tŏ héavĕn, wéll, Ĭ'll téll yŏu ríght nów
Yŏu béttĕr leárn tŏ réad aňd yŏu béttĕr leárn yŏur wŕitīn'
Ŏr yŏu'll névĕr gét tŏ héavĕn 'caŭse yŏu wón't knów hów

Whether we are acquainted with the lyric's melody or not hardly matters. For the words alone, accompanied by their built-in rhythm, instantly conjure up the warning of law-abiding, Bible-reading women, who have nothing better to do than assert their wishes to the naughty Huck. In typical musical-comedy fashion, everybody gets into the act, including Judge Thatcher, several of Huck's friends, some local townspeople, and a chorus of plantation slaves who happen to be nearby. We have no difficulty reading this simple domestic scene as it slowly transforms into a sort of town meeting, with Huck at its very center. We enjoy its unthreatening conflict and stereotypical message—all strangely familiar to us—and perhaps exaggerate the scolding emphasis with which the chorus hammers home its message. We recognize it as the straightforward language of good country folk that necessarily sets the tone for what will follow.

Meeting the Characters on Musical Terms

The scene described above also sets Huck on his journey, and before too long he shares his philosophy with us in a simple but profound musical statement:

Í, Hućklĕbérrў, mé

Sómewhĕre síttiň' uňdeŕnéath soḿe trée

Somewhere maybe fishin'

Maybe someplace sittin' just wishin I was fishin'

Oh, I, Huckleberry, me

Hereby declare myself to be

Nóthiňg évĕr óthĕr thăn

Eẋaćtlў whát Ĭ ám

Repetition, sing-song rhyming, and rhythm characterize Huck's thoughts as he stands alone on stage and confronts us with his wishes and dreams. Notice how the lack of punctuation in this lyric encourages our supplying the right "attack" or "punch" to each of Huck's assertive self-descriptions, as if we, the playreader, were asked to identify with his unpretentious declarations. The message captures Huck's universality, imparts a serious theme of selfhood, and immediately incorporates our participation.

Huck's relationship with his "co-protagonist," Jim, is strikingly captured in a considerably altered rhythmic lyric titled "Muddy Water." Instead of focusing on characters alone, however, the song effectively advances the pace and action of the plot, as both characters "sing as they pole the raft out into the current:"

> Lóok oút fŏr me, óh múddў wátĕr
>
> Yóur mýstĕriés afe deép aňd wíde
>
> And I got a need for goin' someplace
>
> And I got a need to climb upon your back and ride

This duet sung by two powerful vocalists (we do not have the advantage of "hearing" as we playread silently or aloud) demonstrates a thrust and urgency we can hardly ignore. The lyric allows both characters to confront the "mysteries" of the big Mississippi, which is now personified as the means to their salvation. The river itself is a metaphor of life, carrying a white man and a black man, their instinct for survival is all they have in common. Perhaps we envision the raft traveling smoothly across the stage while the sepia-toned etching of the Mississippi achieves an indelible glow behind them, as if to reinforce its special relationship with Huck and Jim. Instead of hearing the lyric's four refrains to the river's "muddy water" as redundant references, they supply the "need for goin' someplace," where there will be no "pain and sorrow / Of no tomorrows comin' in," as Jim so poignantly expresses it.

Advancing the Musical's Theme

Despite the plot complications of both acts, which explore through music and dialogue the colorful characters and incidents from Twain's novel, the friendship between Huck and Jim ultimately supplies the dramatic core of *Big River*. For the success of any musical often focuses on a simple line of action and a cluster of carefully drawn characters.

This is expressed in act 2, when both characters recognize their differences and express them in a song titled "Worlds Apart":

> I see the same stars through my window
> You see through yours
> But we're worlds apart
> Worlds apart

The words strike some very sensitive chords, literally and musically, as the librettist has found his simplest metaphor yet to voice a racial theme that still resounds universally. Nor is there anything "prosaic" or commonplace in the expression of its message: that Huck and Jim are separated by their "blue eyes" and "brown eyes," respectively, a simple biological difference that determines their psychological and social dispositions. We ask ourselves: Can the musical-comedy format capably tackle this controversial theme without seriously jeopardizing its "happily-ever-after" outcome?

Here Jim's eloquent "Free at Last," sung with the Phelps slaves, provides a possible answer, as it imagines a world with equality for all:

> I wish by golly
> I could spread my wings and fly
> And let my grounded soul be free
> For just a little while

When a neighbor restraining Jim "unlocks the chains, which fall to the floor with a crash," it is once again the Mississippi that symbolizes his freedom, like "a long white train / Winding your way away somewhere." Although Jim will follow it north to join his family, he knows that Huck will be "walkin' alongside of me." Rather than face the responsibilities of a civilized person, however, Huck "walks up the steps and toward the river as the stage fades to black." No doubt Mr. Twain would have been very pleased with this stage musical adaptation of his novel; none of the impact of his original work has been lost.

Exploring the Avant-Garde and Other Trends

It remains impossible for any playreader to explore the literature of the theatre without encountering the term *avant-garde* or the string of

labels connected with it. In its designation of selected theatre movements, performance styles, or the individual plays themselves—all of
which have pointed to the possible future direction of the drama—the
contemporary term, often synonymous with "experimental," has perhaps lost some of the urgency and impact it once generated. Nevertheless, it still serves to define and document some very important
trends, such as the aforementioned "alternative" theatre and the
Theatre of the Absurd that, since their categorization as avant-garde,
have comfortably settled into the drama's ever widening mainstream.

What Is Absurd?

A brief reference to the Theatre of the Absurd at an earlier point of
our study has since evolved into a larger, somewhat philosophical body
of dramatic literature, which incorporates the work of a distinguished
circle of American, British, and European playwrights, all of whom are
joined in their efforts to break with traditional forms. In turn they have
provided us with a rich area for investigation. So rather than read these
plays through special lenses, which need not be the case at all, we are now
more prepared to recognize certain styles, in dramatic form and literary
content, that have characterized the more notable avant-garde
"classics."

As some of the practitioners previously discussed have been linked to
the avant-garde, our familiarity with them should facilitate further
observations. These include, in alphabetical order, Albee, Artaud,
Beckett, Brecht, Ionesco, Pinter, and Strindberg. Whether it is
Artaud's anarchistic philosophy, Beckett's "existential" characters,
Albee's anguish, or Pinter's "menacing" predicaments, each has created
characters and actions to reflect the senselessness and absurdity of the
human condition. These characters prompt our own concern for their
feelings of hopelessness: Jerry's inability to communicate (*Zoo Story*);
Vladimir and Estragon's lifetime of waiting (*Godot*); Shen Te's unset-
tling dilemma at the hands of imbecilic gods (*Good Woman*); Ruth's
detached willingness to be sexually compromised by her husband's
family (*The Homecoming*); or Mr. and Mrs. Martin's domestic encounter, alluded to earlier in our study, in which nonsequiturs and gibberish
constitute their shared language (*The Bald Soprano*).

The list boasts numerous indelible images, however, that an alerted
playreader should be prepared to recognize: the pathetic Nagg and
Nell, rising from their garbage cans, hungry for biscuits and love, in

Beckett's *Endgame* (1957); Madame Rosepettle's irreverent traveling from one hotel to another, accompanied by the stuffed corpse of her husband, in Arthur Kopit's *Oh Dad, Poor Dad, Mamma's Hung You in the Closet and I'm Feelin' So Sad* (1962); Berenger's harrowing discovery that the passersby outside his window have all turned into rhinoceroses while he refuses to surrender to the herd instinct in Ionesco's *Rhinoceros* (1959); and the love-hate charade between two maids, who act out their masochistic-sadistic relationship as mistress and servant until their real lady returns, in Jean Genet's *Maids* (1947). (Furthermore, Genet asks the playreader to envision male actors portraying the three "female" characters—a twist that has been successfully realized in actual stage production.)

Whether through character portraits, language, or theme, each of these plays reflects some major aspect of the absurd. By now our sharpened instincts should tell us that such modern or contemporary writers as Shaw, Wilde, O'Neill, Hellman, Shange, and Miller are not classified as absurdists, even though their works may be seriously (or comically) concerned with aspects of the human condition. Not surprisingly, Sam Shepard tends to be omitted from the category; this is not because his dramatic style or themes do not reflect the concerns of the Theatre of the Absurd—which they certainly do—but because Shepard represents the contemporary writer whose daring, frequently unconventional techniques have since been assimilated into the mainstream, causing the avant-garde either to redefine itself or set up newer criteria.

Since we have grown accustomed to searching for signs of *continuity* in the drama, despite the Theatre of the Absurd's deliberate assault on conventionality, the larger questions we should ask ourselves must transcend any fashionable or trendy theatrical movements, including their repercussions. In other words, does this preoccupation with the absurd, or the avant-garde in general, impinge on the world of Sophocles's Oedipus, Shakespeare's Hamlet and Lear, or Chekhov's three sisters, whose painful ennui and futile waiting constitute an inaction that outweighs Beckett? Does our contemporary concern with issues voiced by these absurdists embellish our understanding and appreciation of earlier achievements in the drama? Might we hope to reconcile these conflicting dimensions of character, dramatic structure, language, and theme, or must we merely interpret their contrasts as part of an irreconcilable performance arena? Perhaps as playreaders we should be granted the same freedom given to the contemporary stage director who applies his avant-garde "vision" to the durable Greek tragedians or the flexible Elizabethans, hoping that a certain eclectic approach might enhance the traditional view of the drama. In this way, our imaginations will encompass a multiplicity of visions to serve our own playreading needs.

From Modernism to Postmodernism

Nor should our understanding of Classicism, Romanticism, Realism, and Expressionism—as each term relates to the drama—be daunted by Modernism, a term that encompasses creativity in all areas of art over the past one hundred years; or by Postmodernism, a curious term suggesting that modernism has fulfilled its mission and that a new era has begun. In this so-called "new theatre," practitioners of "experimental" forms—the term *experimental* serving once again as a safe, synonymous substitute for these fancier labels—would like to think that the boundaries between the avant-garde and postmodernism have been clearly defined, which is not the case at all.

Recalling the alternative theatre's "eclecticism," which seeks to be verbally inarticulate in placing a greater emphasis on carefully selected nonverbal codes and images, the responsibility of both spectator and playreader to project their own interpretations on the stage event points to one conclusion: *the form is the content.* This new theatre urgently calls for a reorganization of playreader/performance relationships. Its visual, aural, and verbal images have usurped the more conventional literary drama that has, up to this point, preoccupied our playreading concerns. That is why playwright Robert Wilson, one of the more controversial spokesmen of this new theatre, challenges our playreading sensibilities, so deeply entrenched in logical dramatic structures and traditional character portraits and themes.

Form as Content

Wilson's *Letter for Queen Victoria* (1974) frustrates our expectations with its completely UPPERCASE "script" that offers few clues to its visualization and even more confusing ones to its aural impact. As playreaders, we sorely miss at first the helpful production ingredients that are customarily at our disposal, although we openly respond to the textual ones that, quite fortunately, are strangely abundant and provide a new stage grammar that is pictorialized, coded, and deliberately problematical. Labeled as "operas"—although "operatic" would more appropriately describe their multiple motifs and grandiose stage pictures—Wilson's scripts require a very special and intense analysis. Sound patience, a sharp literary perspective, and, not ironically, some sense of humor will facilitate our playreader's appreciation of his dramatic art.

In *Queen Victoria*, the familiar dramatis personae is reduced to a cast list containing the names of ten performers—rather than the multiple roles they play—and itemizes the musical, choreographic, scenic, costume, and lighting contributors to its four acts. Unlike the literary scripts we are more accustomed to, the collaborative contributions to many postmodern performances are all equally stressed and highlighted, with none subordinate to the other. Representing its single literary center, however, Wilson's script provides the controlling force. Its nonlinear, non-Aristotelian frame also points to the potential reversibility of its parts, which Wilson conveniently lists as "sections." In act 4, section 1, a speaker called "Chinaman" delivers a short speech—a sort of testament of Wilson's purpose—that gives us some clue to the events that have previously occurred:

> STILL, WHEN ONE HAS SPENT SUCH TIME AND DEALT WITH THESE . . . YES, I SUPPOSE YOU MAY CALL THEM INSCRUTABLE SUBTLETIES—ONE CAN BEGIN TO RECOGNIZE THE CONSISTENCIES, THE PATTERNS, OR AS YOU CALL IT, THE MODUS OPERANDI.

And indeed, we quietly adjust to Wilson's "modus operandi," his style of presentation, through which he reveals a set iconography, full of "inscrutable subtleties," so unlike the work of his predecessors and contemporaries but all the more fascinating because of its uniqueness.

Exploring Wilson's Design

We slowly recognize the work's consistencies or "patterns." In act 3, played against a large backdrop "PAINTED WITH A SYMMETRICAL DESIGN OF THE WORDS 'CHITTER' 'CHATTER'," gunshots repeatedly sound off, human bodies fall to the floor, and the slide of an airplane moves from stage left to stage right, while sets of actors, in couples, express familiar statements that seem disconnected, undeveloped, and strangely out of context. One couple exclaims:

1E DID YOU HEAR THAT EVELYN IS GETTING A
   DIVORCE?
2E OH REALLY—HOW DREADFUL

1E YES I DO BELIEVE IT'S IN THE PAPERS
2E IN THE PAPERS!

1E YES
2E HOW DREADFUL

1E DO YOU SEE A CLOUD
2E YES I DO—OH GRACIOUS YOU'RE RIGHT
   THERE IS A CLOUD THERE   ISN'T THERE

1E I DO HOPE IT DOESN'T START RAININ
2E OH THAT WOULD BE SIMPLY TERRIBLE

1E WE REALLY SHOULD SEE MORE OF EACH OTHER
   DON'T YOU THINK
2E YES THAT'S TRUE   IT'S SUCH A PITY THAT WE
   DON'T

ALL: OOOOO   OOHHH   AAHHH
(CURTAIN DOWN)
*(QUEEN VICTORIA ENTERS STAGE LEFT, STOPS IN
PROFILE IN FRONT OF COUPLE 1A AND 2A, AND
SCREAMS THREE TIMES.)*

Our playreading insights once again help us perceive more than we
might as spectators. Aside from its continuity of the absurdist tradition,
Wilson's literal script, devoid of punctuation except for an occasional
question mark, exclamation point, or period, achieves its own internal
rhythm, a pseudo-versification highlighted visually (for us) and aurally
(for the spectator) against the bombardment of "CHITTER" and
"CHATTER," uniformly columnized as backdrop or setting. The
playwright functions in the dual capacity of writer and graphic artist.
But as sound effects, spatial images, and multifunctional actors continually reappear throughout the work's many sections, certain utterances

enable us to recognize and freely associate Wilson's patterns, with or without the traditional meanings we have grown used to in other playreading experiences. Our foremost consideration—that form is content—reminds us, on one hand, to expect nothing beyond what we see and hear, while encouraging us, on the other hand, to interpret Wilson's verbal, visual, and aural images as freely as our imaginations are capable of doing. In short, "meaning" in Wilson's work becomes a purely subjective phenomenon.

Despite its operatic style and multimedia effects, *A Letter for Queen Victoria* is served to us from a proscenium stage—the unadorned box set that so many "alternative" theatre practitioners have eliminated in their efforts to "communalize" both performers and spectators. The unexpected return to this most mainstream of performance spaces isolates Wilson as one of our most eclectic, yet thoroughly original practitioners. He lures us into an experience that is deliberately framed in a familiar stage environment and then dares to communicate with us in his own private, highly theatrical language.

A Summing Up

1. Let the play unfold in your mind's eye. *To read the play in one sitting* meets the realistic expectation of experiencing it from start to finish.

2. Do not expect to integrate all components of the play in an initial reading. A reputable work of dramatic art demands repeated "visits." For example, playreading primarily for *language* may de-emphasize your focus on *characters*, until a second reading brings characters back into perspective.

3. Anticipate ambiguities as an integral part of the playreading experience. If possible, avoid first impressions and hasty conclusions about characters and actions, as they may detract from a fuller, final appreciation of the play.

4. Be sensitive to the rhythms of the play, as you would respond to music. Remember that character dialogue—the play's most distinguishing component—reflects diversity: no character should be perceived exactly like another; no single rhythm should dominate; speech should contrast with silence.

5. Use your playreading imagination to fill in the "missing ingredients" usually provided in a stage production. Recognize that drama is a collaborative art and plays are written to be staged.

6. Enhance your playreading perceptions by viewing the play whenever or wherever possible and transferring all helpful visual and aural impressions to your future playreadings. If a version of the play has been filmed or recorded, rent a video or borrow a library recording to bring you into closer contact with visualizing or hearing the play in its fullest context.

7. Look for continuity. Approach the play under discussion in relation to other works by the same author: For example, how does the playwright's latest play stand up against his earliest?

8. Realize that a playwright's reputation may stand on *one play alone.* Prolific productivity is not mandatory for our appreciation of his art.

9. Consider the play as part of a larger historical framework or as a reflection of its own historical time. Apart from its literary merits, try to incorporate whatever historical, sociological, and psychological dimensions that might enhance your appreciation of the playwright's achievement.

10. Perceive the play as a resonant commodity in which style (i.e., form and content) connects with some earlier literary tradition. Try to associate the play with its antecedents: for example, structure, character types, language, or theme. *A successful play never stands by itself.*

Themes for Analysis: *Mise-en-scène*

Writing about the *mise-en-scène* of any play inevitably requires an expansive consideration of its many aspects and details. In effect, we assume the role of a director who must "block out" his vision of the play as it will unfold before his audience. Although this responsibility necessarily requires a sharp sense of logistics—that is, a clear understanding of the play's many components versus the strategy of an imaginative physical space—it is not unusual for us, as playreaders, to reconstruct or diagram these possibilities.

Describe (or diagram) the *mise-en-scène* for the following plays, making sure to incorporate the patterns, factors, and components suggested by the playwright and by your own imagination to enhance your discussion. Make certain your discussion or illustration provides a *conclusive* investigation of the play's *mise-en-scène:*

1. O'Neill's *Emperor Jones*

   Premise: Protagonist versus his conscience
   Suggested visual pattern: *circular*
   Factors to consider:

   a. the circular journey of Brutus Jones
   b. the hallucinatory nature of his visions
   c. specific production ingredients such as sound effects

2. Shakespeare's *Hamlet*

   Premise: Protagonist as principal actor in his own play
   Suggested visual pattern: *interplay* or *communality*
   Factors to consider:

   a. the shifting monologue versus soliloquy format
   b. the interplay of plot and subplots
   c. Elsinore Castle as an empty stage or, as Hamlet insists, "Denmark's a prison"

3. Hellman's *Little Foxes*

   Premise: Protagonist as active manipulator of her fate
   Suggested visual pattern: *confrontation*
   Factors to consider:

a. the drawing room as center of character interaction
b. the well-made plot structure
c. satellite characters as chorus to principal characters and actions

4. Van Itallie's one-act play *Motel,* from *America Hurrah*

   Premise: Protagonist as transient Everyman on journey toward self-destruction
   Suggested visual patterns: *confrontation* and *communality*
   Factors to consider:

   a. claustrophobic motel room as center for explosive character interaction
   b. atypical production ingredients, such as actors in oversize doll costumes, extraneous lighting and sound effects
   c. hostile integration of actors and audience

5. A variety of fascinating, often puzzling, visual styles characterize Robert Wilson's *Letter for Queen Victoria.* Without decoding the playwright's messages, show how the spatial format of the published script emphasizes form over content.

6. With specific reference to character, action, and language, show how Cole Porter's *Kiss Me Kate* reworks its Shakespearean source.

   Suggested theme: "Cole Porter's Debt to the Classics."

7. Describe how an emphasis on character and language and a de-emphasis of production ingredients enhance the allegorical implications of Michael Bennett's *Chorus Line.*

   Suggested theme: "Allegorical Overtones in *A Chorus Line.*"

GLOSSARY

ACT. A term used to designate the divisions of a play; a block of stage time that reflects a single setting and action, often divided further into "scenes," to reflect multiple settings and actions.

AESTHETIC DISTANCE. The acceptable physical and emotional space established between actor and spectator.

AFRICAN DRAMA. A highly structured non-Western tradition in which ceremony, storytelling, and dance are vital elements. Like the Greek drama, its origins are entirely religious in nature.

ALLEGORY. In the drama, a literary treatment in which the characters are presented through personification or symbolism.

ANALOGOUS ACTIONS. The paralleling of multiple plot structures in any one play.

ANTAGONIST. A major character, also known as the villain, who opposes the protagonist, or hero, of the drama.

ARISTOTLE. A Greek philosopher (384–322 B.C.) whose most popular work, the *Poetics*, has offered Renaissance, neoclassical, and contemporary poets and critics a dynamic set of criteria against which to build and evaluate a literary work (e.g., *Aristotelian concepts*).

ARTICULATION. An acoustical component of character dialogue through which certain sounds of the character's speech reflect aspects of his personality.

AVANT-GARDE. A term that is often synonymous with "experimental," used to suggest the future direction of certain theatrical styles; serves to contrast with *mainstream* or *commercial* drama.

BACKDROP. Sometimes called the scrim, a curtain-like panel located at the back of the stage that provides a panoramic effect.

BLACK COMEDY. Uses the elements of comedy and farce for subversive ends to achieve a certain shock value.

BLOCKING. The characters' stage movements as described by the playwright or reinterpreted by the director.

BOURGEOIS DRAMA. A popular dramatic style of the eighteenth century that focuses on lower-class characters.

BUGAKU. A performance style that preserves the ancient art and music of Japan.

BUNRAKU. The popular puppet theatre of Japan.

CHARACTER. A person in the play who speaks the playwright's dialogue.

CHOREOGRAPHER. The dance director who arranges the dances or patterns of movements in a musical drama.

CHORUS. In the classical drama, actors who speak and move in unison or as one character; in the contemporary musical, used to designate groups of singers or dancers.

CONFIDANT (or confidante [f.]) A supporting character in whom the protagonist confides information that relates to the play's outcome.

CLASSICISM. In literature, a formal arrangement characterized by balance, proportion, and restraint.

CLIMAX. The highest point of the dramatic action, marking a reversal of the protagonist's fortune; also known as the turning point.

CLOSET DRAMA. For technical or literary reasons, a play deemed unproducible, enjoyed solely as a playreading experience instead.

COLLECTIVE THEATRE. An improvisatory theatre process in which the collaborative contributions of the actors and director often relegate the playwright to a subordinate position as "recorder" of the group's rehearsal transactions, which slowly evolve into the performance piece.

COMEDY. In the classical drama, a literary format that celebrates man's triumph over the calamities and downfalls of his life; like tragedy, comedy is rooted in ritual, except that renewal and rebirth fashion its central purpose.

COMIC RELIEF. In a serious play, a device in which the playwright introduces a humorous character or situation to offset the tragic circumstances of the stage action.

COMMEDIA DELL'ARTE. The popular improvisatory performance style of the Italian Renaissance; performed in masks, famous for its influential stock characters.

CONFLICT. In Western drama, the problem or struggle of the characters, leading to the play's climax; an important characteristic of Aristotle's design for tragedy.

CONVENTION. An unrealistic stage device that the spectator agrees to tolerate.

DENOUEMENT. The final unraveling of the protagonist's fate, which follows the turning point in the dramatic action.

DEUS EX MACHINA. Literally translated as "god from the machine"; a convention of Greek drama that rescues the protagonist from his unresolved predicament; in the modern drama, a poorly motivated "easy way out" that often reflects some weakness in plot.

DIDACTICISM. An emphasis on the instructional, rather than entertainment, value of a dramatic work; for example, the didactic Medieval drama.

DIONYSUS. The Greek god of wine and fertility, also known as Bacchus, in whose honor the Western tradition of drama was created.

DIRECTOR. The person who coordinates all aspects of a play production, responsible for the *mise-en-scène.*

DOWNSTAGE. The front area of the conventional box set, closest to the audience.

DRAMATIC IRONY. A device that allows the audience to know more about certain characters and stage actions than the characters themselves do.

DRAMATIS PERSONAE. The characters of the play, traditionally listed as preface to the play text.

DRAMATURGY. The art of writing and producing plays.

ELIZABETHAN DRAMA. Named after the ruling English monarch, Elizabeth I (1533–1603); it provided a unique contribution to the literature of the theatre and was represented by such verse dramatists as Shakespeare and Marlowe.

ENSEMBLE. The interdependent members of an acting company; the emphasis of a group enterprise versus a single performer.

ENVIRONMENTAL THEATRE. A contemporary theatre process that allows both performers and spectators to occupy the same space.

EPIC MODEL. The popular title applied to Bertolt Brecht's dramaturgical and philosophical concepts, as a reaction against Aristotle's *dramatic* model; renowned for its alienation effect, its influence has altered the form and content of the contemporary drama.

EPONYMOUS CHARACTER. The protagonist after whom the play is named.

EXPOSITION. As revealed by the stage characters, any informational background concerning the subsequent events of the play.

EXPRESSIONISM. A theatrical style in which the artist imposes his own personal description of reality on the outside world, rather than letting the outside world impose its reality on him; characterized by distorted physical perspectives and jarring language effects.

FARCE. A style of comedy that excites laughter through the mechanical antics of sight gags, coarse wit, and exaggerated incongruities; a broadly humorous situation.

FEMINIST THEATRE. A thematic response to sociological and pyschological issues that pertain to the welfare of women.

FORESHADOWING. A device that allows the playwright to suggest, early in the action, what may not be fully realized until the final outcome.

FOURTH WALL. The modern concept of an imaginary (fourth) wall between audience and actor, allowing both playwright and actor greater freedom by turning the spectactor into a voyeur.

GREEK DRAMA. Represented by the tragedies of Aeschylus (525–456 B.C.), Sophocles (496–406 B.C.), and Euripides (486–406 B.C.), and the comedies of Aristophanes (450–385 B.C.); a masked drama performed by men; powerful characters, plots, and themes, all presented out-of-doors; marks the beginning of Western drama.

HIGH COMEDY. Intellectual rather than physical comedy; characteristic of Restoration drama and the modern comedy of manners.

IAMBIC PENTAMETER. A popular metrical verse pattern, consisting of five accented beats to each line, that is characteristic of many verse dramas, including the plays of Shakespeare.

ICONOGRAPHY. The vocabulary of visual images and verbal impressions the playwright uses to reveal his dramatic purpose.

IMPROVISATION. Spontaneous dialogue and actions, usually devoid of a literary script.

IRONY. A totally unexpected turn in the play's outcome.

KABUKI. An elaborately costumed, improvisational performance style of Japan, usually performed by male actors.

KATHAKALI. A popular dance-drama of India, in which the threefold process of improvisation, elaboration, and embellishment provides interesting contrast with the Western plot format.

KATHARSIS (CATHARSIS). The desirable emotional cleansing to be experienced on viewing the tragic drama.

KITCHEN-SINK DRAMA. A somewhat unflattering title popularly applied to the unglamorous characters or stage actions of domestic melodramas.

LEGATO. A vocal exchange built on long, smooth-flowing lines.

LIBRETTO. The song lyrics of a musical, as opposed to the musical's book (story line).

MANSIONS. The portable stage sets of medieval drama.

MEDIEVAL DRAMA. The mysteries and moralities of the tenth through fifteenth centuries, with plots based on the stories of the Old and New Testaments; evolved from church ritual and supported by guilds.

MELODRAMA. A playwriting style of the nineteenth century in which the ingredients of tragedy and comedy were interwoven with elements of intrigue and disguise.

MISE-EN-SCÈNE. The arrangement of the drama's many components into an integrated stage picture.

MONOLOGUE. A lengthy stretch of dialogue, spoken by one character to another; a format once popular in the classical drama but less frequently used in the contemporary, realistic theatre.

MOTIF. A recurring element that contributes to the play's central theme.

MOTIVATION. Chiefly applied to stage characters whose inner drives, impulses, and intentions must seem naturally and effortlessly impelled.

MUSICAL PLAY. A theatrical format that blends drama, music, and dance, of which the contribution of music is primary.

NATURALISM. A variation of *realism* in which such factors as environment and heredity determine the actions of stage characters; influential literary style introduced in the late nineteenth century.

NATYASHASTRA. A dramaturgical work, encyclopedic in scope, that incorporates every aspect of Indian dance theatre; compiled between 2 B.C. and 2 A.D. by anonymous collaborators but held to be divinely inspired.

NEOCLASSICISM. A literary style of Restoration drama that revived the classical unities of time, place, and action, which were previously ignored by the Elizabethan playwrights.

NOH. A Japanese performance style that unites dance, song, dialogue, farce, and magic, all within an unplotted structure; significant for its use of masks.

ORCHESTRA. The circular performance space in Greek drama; also refers to the ground floor seating area of most present-day theatres.

PACE. An acoustical component of character dialogue in which the timing and internal rhythms of one character's response are connected meaningfully to those of another; the timing of physical actions as well.

PAGEANT WAGON. Constructed to transport players and stage sets from one town to the next when the medieval cycles expanded and could no longer be contained in the church.

PLOT. The playwright's arrangement of the dramatic action into a cohesive design.

POETRY OF THE THEATRE. The use of vivid prose language to achieve a heightened emotional expression that is often the domain of poetry.

POSTMODERNISM. In the drama, relating to the experimental or "new theatre" forms in which nonverbal codes and images take precedence over spoken language, requiring that the spectator project his own interpretation upon the stage event; that is, the form is the content.

PROSE DRAMA. The nonverse play characteristic of the modern theatre reflecting the realistic speech of lower-class protagonists.

PROTAGONIST. The central figure or hero of the drama.

REALISM. The literary style of the late nineteenth century that tried to show life on stage as it is really lived; that is, with a "slice-of-life" authenticity.

REGIONALISM. An acoustical component of character dialogue that mirrors the origin and social status of the character speaking.

RESTORATION DRAMA. Renowned for witty comedies and sharply etched characters who mirrored the modish intrigues of their courtly audience; a brief but lively duration (1660–1688); featured women in prominent stage roles.

RHYMING COUPLET. A verse pattern in which individual pairs of poetic lines terminate with the identical sound.

ROMAN DRAMA. Famous for the comedies of Plautus (254–184 B.C.) and Terence (190–159 B.C.) and the tragedies of Seneca (3 B.C.–65 A.D.), lasting until the decline of the empire, when the Christian church terminated all forms of theatre.

ROMANTICISM. A popular nineteenth-century literary style that emphasized ego and emotion above everything else, often at the expense of adhering to reality.

SCENE. A popular designation for the smaller units of stage time that mark a change of characters, place, or action and, in a certain consecutive sequence, often constitute a full *act*.

SOLILOQUY. A lengthy speech by one character who stands alone on stage and reveals his private thoughts aloud.

STACCATO. A vocal exchange built on short, choppy rhythms; the opposite of legato.

STAGE LEFT. Designates the left side of the stage from the actor's point of view as he or she faces the spectators.

STAGE RIGHT. Designates the right side of the stage from the actor's point of view as he or she faces the spectators.

STICHOMYTHIA. Fast-paced verbal dueling between characters.

SUBPLOT. A minor story line that is subordinate to the major one.

SUBTEXT. A hidden level of meaning that surfaces slowly through character interaction and subtleties of language.

SURREALISM. In drama, an irrational landscape of the emotions, emphasizing the psychological and subconscious implications of certain stage events.

SYMBOLIC NOMENCLATURE. A device that allows the playwright to affix representative names to his characters.

SYMBOLISM. In drama, the use of language, character, or objects to represent or illuminate something else.

THEATRE OF CRUELTY. The label applied to Antonin Artaud's theatre manifestos, in which he called for a theatre open to risks and violent ends.

THEATRE OF THE ABSURD. A trend in avant-garde drama that uses language and situation to emphasize the philosophical subtext of man's senseless and hopeless condition.

THEME. The representation of a play's central point or underlying message.

TIMBRE. An acoustical component of character dialogue through which the emotional depth of the stage character is revealed.

TRAGEDY. In classical drama, a plot that traces the downfall of its protagonist and arouses pity and terror in the spectator.

TRAGIC FLAW. A weakness in the protagonist that promotes his calamities and makes him sympathetic to us.

TRILOGY. The three-play format, allowing the Greek dramatist some flexibility to follow his protagonist from one setting and action to another but not within the same play.

TROPE. A segment of chanted dialogue from the ritual of the Christian Mass; grew into the full liturgical play and inspired the medieval drama.

UNITIES. Aristotle's rule that drama should tell a single story (action), that it should happen in a single day (time), and be presented in a single scene (place); hence the three unities of action, time, and place.

UPSTAGE. The area of the stage farthest away from the audience; toward the rear or back part of the stage.

VERSE DRAMA. Poetic stage language characterized by rhyme and meter; used popularly in Greek and Elizabethan drama, among other historical periods; declining use in realistic drama.

WELL-MADE PLAY. A tightly structured play that offers its audience a carefully balanced "beginning-middle-end" design; created in the nineteenth century by the French playwright, Eugene Scribe, as a reaction against the formless extravagance of Romanticism.

SUGGESTED READING

The following list of authors and editors has been alphabetized. Their wide-ranging subjects reflect important areas of dramatic theory and practice and will facilitate our reading and writing about drama:

Abramson, Doris. *Negro Playwrights in the American Theatre: 1925-1959*. New York: Columbia University Press, 1969.

Aristotle, *The Poetics*. (Transl. S. H. Butcher). New York: Hill and Wang, 1986.

Barton, John. *Playing Shakespeare*. New York: Methuen, 1984.

Betsko, Kathleen, and Koenig, Rachel. *Interviews with Contemporary Women Playwrights*. New York: Beech Tree Books, 1987.

Chinoy, Helen, and Jenkins, Linda. *Women in American Theatre*. New York: Crown Publishers Inc., 1981.

Clark, Barrett. *European Theories of the Drama*. (With a Supplement on the American Drama). New York: Crown Publishers, 1947.

Dean, Alexander, and Carra, Laurence. *Fundamentals of Play Directing*, Revised edition. New York: Holt, Rinehart and Winston, 1965.

Esslin, Martin. *The Theatre of the Absurd*. New York: Doubleday and Co., 1961.

Fergusson, Francis. *The Idea of a Theater*. New York: Doubleday and Co., 1949.

Gassner, John. *Masters of the Drama*. New York: Dover Publications, Inc., 1954.

Hayman, Ronald. *British Theatre Since 1955: A Reassessment.* New York: Oxford University Press, 1979.

Jones, Robert Edmond. *The Dramatic Imagination.* New York: Theatre Arts Books, 1941.

Kennedy, Scott. *In Search of African Theatre.* New York: Charles Scribner's Sons, 1973.

Keyssar, Helene. *Feminist Theatre.* New York: Grove Press, 1985.

Kirby, Michael (ed.). *The New Theatre: Performance Documentation: An Anthology.* New York: New York University Press, 1974.

Kott, Jan. *Shakespeare Our Contemporary.* New York: W. W. Norton & Co., 1964.

Mordden, Ethan. *Broadway Babies: The People Who Made the American Musical.* New York: Oxford University Press, 1983.

Nagler, A. M. *A Source Book in Theatrical History.* New York: Dover Publications, Inc., 1952.

Roberts, Vera Mowry. *On Stage: A History of Theatre.* New York: Harper & Row, 1962.

Schechner, Richard. *Environmental Theatre.* New York: Hawthorn Books, Inc., 1973.

Scott, A. C. *The Theatre in Asia.* New York: Macmillan Publishing Co., 1972.

Seltzer, Daniel. *The Modern Theatre: Readings and Documents.* Boston: Little, Brown and Company, 1967.

Shank, Theodore. *American Alternative Theater.* New York: Grove Press, 1982.

Simonson, Lee. *The Stage Is Set.* New York: Theatre Arts Books, 1963.

Stuart, Donald Clive. *The Development of Dramatic Art*. New York: Dover Publications, 1960.

Wager, Walter. *The Playwrights Speak*. New York: Dell Publishing Co., 1967.

Wandor, Michelene. *Carry On, Understudies: Theatre and Sexual Politics*. New York: Routledge & Kegan Paul, 1981.

Willett, John. (ed.) *Brecht on Theatre*. New York: Hill and Wang, 1964.

Wills, J. Robert. (ed.) *The Director in a Changing Theatre*. California: Mayfield Publishing Co., 1976.

Wilson, Robert. *The Theater of Images*. New York: Harper & Row, 1984.

The following sampling of play collections is arranged in chronological order and offers a variety of representative texts, all essential for a fuller understanding and appreciation of the drama:

Corrigan, Robert (ed.) *Classical Comedy: Greek and Roman*. New York: Applause Theatre Book Publishers, 1987.

Roche, Paul. (transl.) *The Oedipus Plays of Sophocles*. New York: The New American Library, 1958.

————. *The Orestes Plays of Aeschylus*. New York: The New American Library, 1963.

————. *Three Plays of Euripides*. New York: W. W. Norton & Co., 1974.

Adams, Joseph Quincy. (ed.) *Chief Pre-Shakespearean Dramas*. New York, AMS Press, 1952.

Baskervill, Charles, Heltzel, Virgil, and Nethercot, Arthur. (eds.) *Elizabethan and Stuart Plays*. New York: Holt, Rinehart & Winston, 1963.

Harbage, Alfred. (ed.) *The Complete Pelican Shakespeare*. New York: Viking Press, 1969.

Nettleton, George, and Case, Arthur. (eds.) *British Dramatists from Dryden to Sheridan*. Carbondale: Southern Illinois University Press, 1969.

Coyle, William, and Damaser, Harvey G. (eds.) *Six Early American Plays: 1798-1890*. Ohio: Charles E. Merrill Publishing Co., 1968.

Clark, Barrett (ed.) *World Drama: 26 Unabridged Plays*, Vol I., New York: Dover Publications, 1933.

———. *World Drama: 20 Unabridged Plays*, Vol. II., New York: Dover Publications, 1933.

Gassner, John (ed.) *Best Plays of the Early American Theatre: From the Beginning to 1916*. New York: Crown Publishers, 1967.

———. *Best American Plays: 1918-1958*. New York: Crown Publishers, 1961.

———. *Best American Plays: Third Series, 1945-51*. New York: Crown Publishers, 1952.

———. *Best American Plays: Fourth Series, 1952-1957*. New York: Crown Publishers, 1958.

———. *Best American Plays: Fifth Series, 1958-1963*. New York: Crown Publishers, 1958.

———. *A Treasury of the Theatre: from Henrik Ibsen to Eugene Ionesco*. New York: Simon & Schuster, 1961.

Cerf, Bennett, and Cartnell, Van. *24 Favorite One-Act Plays*. New York: Dolphin Press, 1963.

Dukore, Bernard F., and Gerould, Daniel C. *Avant Garde Drama: A Casebook 1918-1939*. New York: Thomas Y. Crowell Co., 1976.

Hatch, James V. (ed.) *Black Theater USA: 45 Plays by Black Americans, 1947-1974*. New York: The Free Press, 1974.

Kriegel, Harriet (ed.) *Women in Drama: An Anthology*. New York: New American Library, 1975.

Moore, Honor (ed.) *The New Women's Theatre: Ten Plays by Contemporary American Woman*. New York: Vintage Books, 1977.

Marranca, Bonnie. *The Theatre of Images*. New York: PAJ Publications, 1977.

also:

Lal, P. *Great Sanskrit Plays in Modern Translation*. New York: New Directions, 1964.

Keene, Donald. (ed.) *Twenty Plays of the Nō Theatre*. New York: Columbia University Press, 1970.